BUILT FOR BATTLE!

BUILT FOR BATTLE!

The strategy of Jesus for the Last Days

CHRIS HILL

𝒞 𝓛 Publications

$\mathcal{C}\mathcal{L}$ Publications

28 Thorney Road, Capel St Mary, Suffolk IP9 2LH

Copyright © Christopher Hill

First Published 2014

Cover design and print production for the publisher by Gipping Press Ltd., Needham Market, Suffolk IP6 8NZ

ISBN 978-0-9928067

CONTENTS

Chapter One

Confrontation on the Golan Heights

It might be disputed land, but Lindy and I like the Golan Heights. It is a fascinating, volcanic plateau in the north east of Israel that rises above the villages and kibbutzim around the Sea of Galilee. Whoever controls the Golan controls northern Israel.

When we leave our lakeside Hotel, we approach the Golan from the south eastern corner of the lake. The driver guides the bus up the narrow, winding way that climbs above the River Yarmuk until the road levels off and the massive plateau stretches out before us.

This is rugged, volcanic Golan, known in the Bible as Bashan, a place of fertile pasturelands for well nourished livestock *(Deuteronomy 32:14; Psalm 22:12; Ezekiel 39:18)* and majestic oak forests *(Isaiah 2:13; Ezekiel 27:6)*.

Mighty Mount Hermon towers over the northern extremity of the Golan and when it is crowned with glistening winter snow it sings out a promise of abundant, life giving water for the Jordan.

Nestling in the foothills of the mountain is a natural spring that gushes from beneath the rock and plunges down into the Huleh Valley. Cameras click to record the beauty of the place.

However, the beautiful spring has been associated with terrible things. In Old Testament times, the area was known as Baal-Hermon. It is located in the shadow of the mountain and it was also under the dark shadow of Baal-worship – child sacrifice and all. Great evil was perpetrated here. When the land was overrun by the Greeks, they suggested that the gushing spring was the place where the god Pan was born. A shrine was created and Pan-worship overlaid the worship of Baal. The Greeks renamed the place Panyas.

When the Romans came they wanted to establish their religious dominance by erecting a splendid temple in honour of Jupiter, chief among the Roman gods.

After the death of Herod the Great, the Golan Heights were ruled by Herod's son, Philip. He wished to ingratiate himself with the Roman Emperor and so right there, adjacent to the shrines of Baal, Pan and Jupiter, he built a temple in honour of Caesar himself and renamed the town Caesarea Philippi. That is the name used by Matthew and Mark in their gospel accounts.

Caesarea Philippi, although a beautiful and important Roman city, straddling a great trading route that connected North Africa with the Persian Gulf, had become a satanic stronghold: one demonic religion had been overlaid on the top of another.

Yet it was in this surprising setting that God gave the apostle Peter a most astonishing revelation concerning our Lord Jesus Christ.

Who is Jesus?

Matthew 16:13-20 describes the event. Jesus had left the shores of the Sea of Galilee and was heading for the heights of Hermon. There Peter, James and John would see him transfigured in the presence of Moses and Elijah. As Jesus and the disciples climbed up the ancient 'Road to Damascus' they passed through Caesarea Philippi. Here Jesus paused to ask them a searching question: *'Who do you say that I am?'* Peter answered, *'You are the Christ, the Son of the living God!'*

'CHRISTOS' is the Greek translation of the Hebrew word *'MESHIACH'*, meaning Messiah, one who is anointed.

Jesus' response elevates Peter's outburst to the most glorious heights: *'Blessed are you Simon son of Jonah, for this was not revealed to you by man, but by my Father in heaven.'*

Peter's words came straight out of Heaven, borne on the breath of the Holy Spirit. Is it not extraordinary that such revelation could be given by God in a place with a history of paganism like Caesarea Philippi? I am so encouraged by that. It tells me that there is no situation so bad that my Father is incapable of pouring revelation about Jesus through one of his disciples! Let's be encouraged. No doubt you feel that there are circumstances of life where it is difficult (if not impossible) for you to speak a word of revelation about Jesus.

The episode at Caesarea Philippi shows otherwise! Praise the Lord! If God can give revelation of Jesus through a person like Peter and in such a haunt of demons, he can do it *anywhere*!

The One Foundation
Jesus then continued and said, *'I tell you that you are Peter (Gk: PETROS) and on this rock (Gk: PETRA) I will build my Church.'*

Here is revelation indeed. Our Lord establishes that the Church he will build must have a rock foundation. But which rock? Some have suggested he was referring to Peter and that the Church would be established on *him*. This was far from our Lord's meaning. The rock he refers to is the *revelation from heaven* that Peter spoke out as direct and personal communication from God's Throne Room: *'You are the Messiah, the Son of the living God.'*

The Greek word *PETROS* means a small stone: a pebble or piece of grit. The word *PETRA* means a mighty rock. Jesus would certainly not intend to build his Church on a 'pebble', however special it was!

The mighty rock is none other than Jesus himself. Father God revealed him as Messiah and as his Son. As we have seen, the Hebrew word *MESHIACH* means 'one who is anointed'. In Bible times they anointed kings and priests. Heaven's revealed title given through Peter shows that Jesus is the King of Kings and our Great High Priest. The theological weight of this is massive.

When taken together with *'You are the Son of the living God'* – a clear statement of divinity – we have three truths about Jesus that provide the most glorious exposition of his nature and his redeeming work: Jesus is our Great High Priest, he is the King of Kings, he is God the Son. As Paul put it in *1 Corinthians 3:11, 'For no-one can lay any foundation other than the one already laid, **which is Jesus Christ.'***

It is the only sure foundation of the Church. There is no other. Jesus Christ is the unique foundation. Alter or add to that foundation and a different church rises up. A hybrid monster that is an offence to God. It's that serious.

The Master Builder
'On this rock I will build my Church.' No one but Jesus builds *his* Church! He is the self-confessed master builder.

They called Jesus the *'carpenter' (Mark 6:3)*. But his manual work involved more than that. The Greek word, *TEKTON*, means builder as well as carpenter. Jesus built with stone and wood. He was principally a stone mason. There may well have been people in Sepphoris and the villages of Upper Galilee who dwelt in homes built by 'Joseph and Sons', master builders from Nazareth!

In his teaching, our Lord had little to say about the carpentry trade. He spoke of his yoke fitting well *(Matthew 11:30)* and made reference to a wooden beam *(Matthew 7:3),* and that's about all. But he was often speaking about buildings and working with stone *(Matthew 7:24-26; Luke 12:18; 14:28; 20:17; etc.)*.

On one occasion one of the disciples called his attention to the enormous stones used to build Herod's Temple, no doubt because he knew Jesus would be interested *(Mark 13:1-2)*. I'm sure he was!

Built for battle!
On this immense occasion, Jesus went on to define the primary ministry of the Church he would build. It will surprise many … and frighten not a few!
'On this rock I will build my Church, and the gates of Hades will not overcome it.'

This is the first time Jesus refers to his Church and so we must take it as a formative statement, showing his firm expectation of us. *'The gates of Hades will not overcome it.'*

The Bible version I have used here is the *New International Version*, but in order to get the full weight of Jesus' words we need to look carefully at the original Greek text. It would be strange indeed if Jesus had implied that literal gates could overcome anything! I have yet to see a set of gates lifting off their hinges and attacking someone!

So what are we to make of it? In Old Testament times, people went to the gate of a city to find a judge. If they were pursuing a just cause, the appropriate authorities were to be found there. So the word 'gates' should be considered as representing 'authorities'.

Second, the word *'Hades'*. The actual word in the Greek text is *'hell'*, the dominion of Satan.

The phrase *'the gates of hell'* means malevolent devil-inspired authorities: the principalities and powers, sometimes demonic, sometimes human.

Third, the phrase that follows it. The Greek words mean two things: *'will not overcome it'* and also *'will not prove stronger than it'*. The Greek really does mean *both*!

So Jesus said that the first priority for his great Church would be engaging the authorities of the enemy both in terms of defence and attack. That is spiritual warfare.

The great snag with warfare is that the decision to go to war is never left to the individual soldier. Our King has made the decision. Jesus has declared war on Satan and so we are pitched straight into it, like it or not.

In a regular war some might opt out as conscientious objectors. In the war between Jesus and Satan there is no such loophole. Refusal to fight means instant defeat by the enemy.

So we have great need to be trained for battle. Untrained troops stand little chance against a determined and vicious foe. Praise the Lord that he has provided us with a clear and straightforward training manual. It is to the Bible that we look for help. How do we defend ourselves against the shock-troops of Satan? How do we attack and take ground from him?

These are questions that demand the closest attention.

Chapter Two

The Jesus Way

For many Christians, spiritual warfare is a fringe activity of the Church. Something to be avoided if possible. Certainly something that is outside Christian orthodoxy.

Such thinking is sadly mistaken.

'HMS Belfast'
This mighty cruiser lies anchored in the Thames, close by the Tower of London, a neighbouring bastion of English power. The 'Belfast' saw active service in World War II and members of its crew of 800 distinguished themselves with great courage. She was an escort on the Russian convoys, was engaged in the Battle of the North Cape and was a bombarding force at D-Day on the 6th June 1944. HMS Belfast continued to be a formidable Cruiser throughout the forties and in the Korean War she fired so many salvoes that she wore out her twelve 6-inch guns! Her additional fire-power included eight 4-inch guns and twelve anti-aircraft Bofors. Her armour was 4.5 inches thick! After a distinguished career, HMS Belfast sailed for home on the 27th September 1952, having fired her guns in anger for the last time. The sailors are long gone and today thousands of tourists swarm over the mighty ship, admiring her majestic

lines, awestruck by her arms, impressed by memories of greatness.

But for all her impressiveness there is something pathetic about the great ship. It's all history. Her guns are not only silent: they are 'bunged up': their firing mechanisms removed. The 'Belfast' no longer has the ability to engage Britain's enemies. Memories are all that are left.

Warfare in the Golan Heights

When Jesus had his amazing exchange with Peter up in the northern Golan Heights at Caesarea Philippi *(Matthew 16:13-20)*, he revealed that his Church would be constructed on a firm foundation: the revelation that he is Messiah (King of kings and Great High Priest) and the divine Son of the Father. So, as the hymn writer put it, "Christ is made the sure foundation!" Woe betide anyone who messes with that! *"No other foundation can any man lay other than the one already laid, which is Jesus Christ" (1 Corinthians 3:11).*

The Church built on that solid foundation has a clear mandate from Jesus: *"I will build my Church and the gates (authorities) of Hades (literally, hell) will not overcome it (or prove stronger than it)" (Matthew 16:18).*

This is fighting talk! The statement shows that our function in this world can be described as 'warfare'. Jesus speaks of his Church attacking Satan's evil forces and also standing firm against them.

For many of us, spiritual warfare is the last thing on our minds. And even when we acknowledge the reality of it, it's often seen as the activity of extremists, not to say fanatics!

Mention spiritual warfare in many Christian circles and the response you may get is "No, thank you! All that stuff is for the loony brigade – *we* are *normal* Christians!"

The truth, however, is that, according to Jesus, warfare is the 'normal' and regular activity of his Church! So not to be engaging Satan in spiritual warfare would appear to be missing the point.

Some consign spiritual warfare to the historic Church, particularly to the New Testament. The apostles were engaged in all manner of things that have passed out of the Church and as regards spiritual warfare, many would say, "A good thing too!"

So in terms of spiritual warfare, to compare many modern churches with New Testament churches is rather like seeing 'HMS Belfast' today in comparison with that self-same ship engaging the enemy with all guns blazing. "Fings ain't what they used to be!"

Attacking Satan's strongholds
Jesus told his apostles, *"Follow me"*. They did. Absolutely. Their discipleship was based upon a simple premise. They did what he said and they did what he did. Disciples of Christ follow him now as then. Why should it be different?

So to what extent did Jesus engage Satan's kingdom in spiritual warfare during the years of his ministry here? Was it on the particular occasions when he ministered deliverance from demons? No, indeed.

Our Lord invaded Satan's kingdom on a daily basis and successfully defended himself when attacked. The two aspects of warfare – attack and defence – are writ large over the Gospel accounts.

Taking ground from the enemy's territory
So how did Jesus attack Satan's kingdom? How did he invade it and release captives? He did it through his regular ministry. He raised the dead; he healed the sick and he cast out demons. His words of knowledge unlocked people's lives [like the woman at the well at Sychar *(John 4:17)*]; and so did his words of wisdom [as when he used a Roman coin to teach on tax *(Matthew 22:20-21)*]. Through the prophetic word Jesus took the Scriptures and drove them into people's consciousness with the dynamic power of the Spirit to bring fulfilling revelation. In all these ways our Lord was taking ground from the enemy. He was attacking Satan's kingdom. His supreme victory was the Cross. Death itself was snatched from Satan's grip.

So how do we relate to this?

Main stream ministry
The forces at work in this dark world need to be confronted and engaged through the ministry of Jesus Christ in his corporate body – his Church. That is the exciting adventure to

which every disciple of Jesus Christ is called and for which he is equipped through the gifts of the Holy Spirit.

True spiritual warfare is therefore waged in mission as we evangelise and bring life to the dead, heal the sick, restore sight to the blind, give freedom to the captives and revelation to the unaware.

This places spiritual warfare right at the centre of normal Church life. It is not the prerogative of the few, but is intended to be the regular activity of every member.

We need to learn how to handle our spiritual gifts by strict obedience to the Scriptures, our only manual. It is enough, praise the Lord.

So to say, "The gifts of the Holy Spirit are not for today" is rather like saying, "Christian Mission has no part in the life of the Church". Few would actually realise it, but it is the inevitable consequence of relegating the spiritual gifts to former times.

Without exercising spiritual gifts, a church is closely similar to HMS Belfast. Not as it once *was*, but as it now *is:* yesterday's magnificent warrior: today's museum to glories past.

Resisting the enemy
Warfare comprises attack *and* defence. If the ministry gifts of Jesus let loose through his Church provide us with attack weaponry, what of defence?

Here we are indebted to the apostle Paul. In *Ephesians 6:10-18,* he described the believer standing in the Armour of God. Some suggest that in this famous passage he describes the believer *attacking* the devil's principalities and powers. More careful examination shows the emphasis to be on defence and not attack. A key word that recurs is "stand": Paul is describing the soldier standing his ground when under attack *(Ephesians 6:11, 13 and 14).*

Our stand is against the rulers, principalities and powers of this dark world and over and beyond that, the spiritual forces of evil in the heavenly realms. One major battle front is here in the world but we must be alert to the insidious and more secret battle front beyond this world. The battle on both fronts is fought in the Spirit by wielding the *Sword* of the Spirit – the word of God. It is the only weapon Paul mentions here. Prayer in the Spirit is our means of communication with our Commander, but the Word of God is our only weapon.

How did Jesus do it?
How did our Lord defend himself against the attack of the enemy? His victory over temptation in the Wilderness is a clear example. According to *Matthew 4:1-11 (*also *Mark 1:12-13* and *Luke 4:1-13),* every attack by Satan was repulsed by Jesus wielding the Sword – the written Word.

The crucifixion must surely be the most extreme example of Satan attacking our Lord. There could never be a worse one. How did Jesus defend himself with such triumphant success? By being thoroughly prepared. How so?

Hebrews 12:2-4 provides us with a compelling insight: *"Let us fix our eyes on Jesus, the author and perfecter of our faith, who, for the joy set before him, endured the cross, scorning its shame and sat down at the right hand of the throne of God"*.

Note also the following statement, *"Consider him who endured such opposition from sinful men, so that you will not grow weary and lose heart. In your struggle against sin, you have not yet resisted to the point of shedding your blood."*

The writer is describing disciples of Christ called to defend themselves when under attack. He parallels it with the experience of Jesus on the cross. Words like "endured", "opposition", "struggle" and "resist" are words describing *defence* against a vicious foe.

How do we take our example from Jesus?

The writer to the Hebrews says we must *"fix our eyes on Jesus ... who for the joy set before him endured the cross"*. He was strengthened to endure the most terrible and vicious attack perpetrated by Satan and those who were his willing accomplices by something described as *"the joy set before him"*. What was this joy?

We cannot be certain. Was it the prospect of returning to his Father's throne-room? Was it the glorious awareness of what his death was accomplishing in offering his life as a ransom for many? No doubt both are true.

But we are provided with an additional insight in *Luke 9:30-31*. Our Lord was transfigured (most likely on Mount Hermon).

Moses and Elijah came to him from beyond the grave. The encounter was witnessed by Peter, James and John. Moses is associated with the Law given at Sinai while Elijah is the great prophet. The Law contains vast amounts of wonderful Messianic "types" (Noah's Ark, the Passover Lamb, the High Priest, etc. etc.) while the Prophets contain vast amounts of prophecy concerning the coming Messiah both as the Suffering Servant and the glorious King.

In other words, Moses and Elijah were exercising their ministries in preparing Jesus for his "departure" (Greek: *EXODOS*) from this world to the next one. They were ministering the Word of God to Jesus: reminding him of the immensity of the biblical revelation concerning his death, resurrection and ascension. To be filled with those Scriptures provided Jesus with the means to defeat the onslaught of Satan. They strengthened him to become the one sacrifice for the sin of the world. The Mighty Victor would come roaring through the very worst attack of Satan, Sword in hand!

Soldiers of Christ, arise!
The example of Jesus should surely demonstrate that spiritual warfare is the principal work of true disciples. There is no opting out on conscience grounds in the Kingdom of God.

Let's take the fight to the enemy. He's been pushing us around for far too long. There's a war to be won and a standard to be raised. Jesus the Conqueror reigns! To him be the glory!

Chapter Three

Know your weapons!

Front line soldiers confronted with a vicious enemy need confidence in their weapons and have the ability to use them.

Presented with the stark truth that we are called to warfare, some of us react, "I never signed on for *this!*" Problems, attack, pain or persecution are not on our agendas!

In some way we have got the impression that when things go against us – when we are confronted with crisis or challenge – it is an indication that something has gone horribly wrong and we must have wandered outside the will of God and therefore his protection.

The problem can be fed by well meaning preachers who tell us that once we come to Christ all our problems are at an end and it should be joy and felicity all the way! Well, it ain't like that … at all!

People who think like that have not read much in the Bible. *Hebrews 11* provides a great cavalcade of the faithful from Old Testament times. They stood strong in the storms that engulfed them. Indeed, the writer makes a telling comment in verse *13*: *"All these people were still living by faith when they died."*

It's an extraordinary testimony and serves to inspire us, particularly when we are faced with challenges of many kinds. Those saints of old stood firm under fierce pressure.

We can too. At any rate that seems to be the whole point of *Hebrews 12:1-12.* Standing strong through the storm is made even more possible for Christians because *we* are born again and have received the Holy Spirit.

If Jesus is to be believed, conflict and trouble must be expected when we are determined to be his disciples. His clearest warning is *John 16:33 "In this world you will have trouble."* That's plain enough. Thank the Lord for what follows! *"But take heart! **I** have overcome the world."*

All leave is cancelled forthwith!
Disciples of Christ are called to be warriors. Jesus said as much when he laid down the foundation for his Church's engagement with the world. In *Matthew 16:18* we read *"I will build my Church and the gates (authorities) of Hades (literally, hell) will not overcome it (or prove stronger than it)."*

So warfare is a major part of our Lord's clear expectation for the Church that would exist in the world: first, defending itself successfully against the devil and all his works and second, aggressively attacking the devil's kingdom and doing that successfully too.

It is the vision Jesus has for the Church *he* would build: the true Church, distinct from the apparent and apostate Church.

There is a massive difference between the two. According to *Matthew 16:16-18,* our Lord spoke of a Church built upon the reality of his being Messiah (anointed priest and king) and the divine Son. The great challenge for us is to ensure that we are part of *that* Church and not some pretended alternative.

Strategy matters
In any and every conflict, battle strategy is critical. Good weapons are vital and so is the ability to use them. We need armour that does its job, a clear campaign strategy, confidence in the command structure, good communication with HQ and strong personal discipline. A casual approach courts certain disaster. Troops have to be trained and discipline begins with discipline over oneself.

So as we search the Scriptures we find a continual emphasis on discipleship in the training school of Jesus. He trained the disciples rigorously and at times was confrontational to the point where he really scared them. On one occasion his words were so challenging that many pulled back and left him (*John 6:66*). That is the test: when the going gets tough it tests to see who will stick with him: who is truly our Lord's disciple and who is simply a camp-follower. With a relatively tiny number of genuine apprentices – men willing to follow him and take to heart and apply everything he taught – Jesus was able to establish his Church and it was capable of defeating Satan's forces and defending itself against them. Warfare is regular service in the Church that Jesus builds.

Jesus attacked Satan's kingdom and took territory from him as he exercised his ministry. It is so for the true Church.

When we were baptised in the Holy Spirit, gifts were given that have a solemn purpose: they are for plundering Satan's kingdom and releasing his prisoners. Jesus did that all the time. Every aspect of his ministry can be viewed in that way.

When he preached in Nazareth shortly after the Spirit came upon him and filled him at the Jordan, he quoted from *Isaiah 61:1-2*, demonstrating his awareness of what he would be doing for the next three years: *"The Spirit of the Lord is upon me, because he has anointed me to preach good news to the poor. He has sent me to proclaim freedom for the prisoners and recovery of sight to the blind, to release the oppressed (lit. those who are bruised), to proclaim the year of the Lord's favour."*

So if a believer refuses to use the gifts of the Spirit (or even acknowledge them) it is clear that he is not prepared to plunder Satan's kingdom. Jesus did it that way: so should we.

For use and not for ornament!
There is a danger that we treat the gifts (especially tongues) as little more than a confirmation that we have been baptised in the Spirit. A kind of "badge" showing we belong! But the gifts of the Holy Spirit are given to us for *use*. I sometimes ask people who claim to be baptised in the Holy Spirit, "Do you speak in tongues?" Their usual response is "Yes, I *can!*" But that wasn't the question! I asked, *"Do* you speak in tongues?" Another matter altogether. And what applies to tongues also applies to the other gifts.

There is a big difference between ability to do something and actually doing it. I use the example of tongues, but it applies to all the gifts. Non-use of the gifts means peace for Satan's kingdom, leaving his forces to run rampant. Is that what we want? Is it what Jesus wants?

In churches where the gifts of the Spirit are believed in and preached about they may still be rarely exercised. Satan loves that! He's even more delighted when they are not exercised by Christians when they are *out in the world*. It is highly significant that Jesus healed the sick, cast out demons, spoke the prophetic word, gave words of wisdom and knowledge as he was tramping the roads and encountering people in the market places. He did not perform miracles of healing and revelation only in synagogues. He took his ministry to the world.

John 4 recounts a great moment of victory by the well in the heart of a West Bank village called Sychar. The situation was cracked open when our Lord had a word of knowledge about a certain Samaritan woman's domestic circumstances. Jesus challenged her head on when he told her she had seen off five husbands and was now living with yet another man! How did Jesus know that? It was a clear word of knowledge given right there in the centre of the village. Ministry on the road was normal in the life of Jesus: his use of the gifts was not limited by setting: homes and public places, country roads and city streets, hillside and lakeside were all locations where Satan's kingdom suffered one thumping defeat after another! Prisoner after prisoner set free! Jesus was ministering the gifts! Hallelujah!

Does that excite you? Does it provoke you? I hope so, because at the moment there appears to be comparatively little genuine ministry out in the battlefield. How many of us ever expect a word of wisdom when we are going about our daily work? When we are confronted with a technical problem, do we look to the Lord for a word of knowledge? When we can't understand a particularly tricky piece of information, do we ask the Lord for and expect to receive a word of wisdom? Are healing and deliverance or a prophetic word ever even on the agenda as we rub shoulders with people in Tesco's?

It is such an alien idea that it will sound almost like a joke to some readers. But do we need to reassess? Spiritual warfare is not an option it is a necessity, and in order to fight we need weapons. The gifts of the Holy Spirit are the weapons Jesus used and so it is highly probable that ours will be the same. Do you think that's fair comment? If so, there is a job to be done.

Combat training required, please!

One of the greatest needs in churches is combat training. Jesus adopted a discursive training programme with the disciples. The clear impression I get from reading the gospels is that he taught them from the Scriptures, he talked it through with them, he demonstrated how to do it, sorted out their personal problems and then he sent them out to put it all into practice. When they returned he reviewed the situation, showed them how to improve and then sent them out to do it again.

I think that is what happened. Jesus did not sit them down and lecture them for hours to fill their heads with information (however good): he *trained* them to do what he did and his method was very rabbinical – he taught them in a tutorial setting in which they were free to question him and offer their own views for him to confirm or confound! He trained them to such a level that he was able to promise that once the Holy Spirit came on them they would be able to do the same kind of things he was doing even though he would then be absent from them. He even went so far as to say they would have a far more extensive ministry than he had himself because he was returning to the Father and would therefore send the Holy Spirit into them, creating a corporate body capable of going into all the world (*John 14:12*).

It is a far cry from what passes for normal church practice today. But need it stay like that? Jesus hasn't changed. The Holy Spirit is still the same. The Father still delights to give the Holy Spirit to those that ask him. We are still the corporate Body of Christ.

So where is the problem?

Perhaps it lies in a neglect of disciple *training*. After all, Jesus did command us to go and *make disciples*. Disciples are different from converts. As we have seen, those that accompanied Jesus learned from him. It was intimate and thorough. They became like him. There was no room for a casual approach. He was deadly serious about seeing them changed and equipped.

Is that where things are breaking down? Are we willing to be discipled in the New Testament sense? Are we being encouraged to be like Jesus in his character and in his ministry?

It's time for action.

Chapter Four

Cowards may go home!

"Based on 'is performance in the television debate last night, I'm gonna vote for *'im!*"

How depressing is *that*? Trial by television has truly arrived. Personality is everything. It is a symptom of the trivialising of all things important in our nation. That includes the Bible. If viewers form their opinion on Christianity from what they are fed through the 'screen', it is no wonder they are so ignorant of the truth, and instead believe lies.

War in the air

I'm not entirely sure what Paul meant, but it intrigues me that one of his descriptions of Satan is as the *"Prince of the power of the air" (Ephesians 2:2)*. Could this apply in part to the waves that bring various forms of media through the air into our homes? Whether it's TV, radio or Internet, Satan appears to control a huge proportion of it, such that even so-called 'Christian broadcasting' is, to a massive extent, devoid of the Spirit and thoroughly unbiblical.

It all serves to demonstrate that Spiritual Warfare is a far bigger issue than we think. Our enemy invades our space on all fronts, and yet Jesus promised the disciples, *"I will build my church and the gates of Hades shall not overcome it"*.

A fuller and clearer rendering of that statement is, *"I will
build my church and the authorities of hell shall not overcome
it (or be able to stand against it)."*

This extraordinary, prophetic statement made by Jesus is
either true or it isn't. I choose to believe that it's true (I'm
sure you do too). So what does it mean in the present debate?
Surely it means there is neither rhyme nor reason why satanic
power should invade Christian homes with such success. Our
Father gives us the weapons we need to destroy the forces of
the devil and also to defend ourselves against them: so why
are we so reluctant to use them?

It's a question that requires an honest answer. If I do not take
authority, shall we say, over evil things entering my home
(and therefore my life) I have a lot to answer for. Why am I so
casual about what I watch on television and what I allow my
family members to watch? Why do I not shout the alarm and
exercise my right to switch the 'tele' off or even throw it into
the fishpond?

Cowardice in the field?
I think it's because I'm something of a coward. The
implications of taking such drastic action would immediately
point me out as ridiculous in the eyes of many people I know
and like – including some Christians. I prefer to be well
thought of, not branded a crank.

There is a comment in *Revelation 21:8* that caught my eye the
other day. In fact it has shaken me considerably and has

caused me to examine myself pretty closely and in doing so I have found something I don't like very much.

The verse is set within the context of life in the New Jerusalem. A stark contrast is drawn between overcomers and those who are not. The Lord, the Alpha and Omega, is speaking and he says, *"But the cowardly, the unbelieving, the vile, the murderers ... their place will be in the fiery lake of burning sulphur. This is the second death."*

I was struck by that word, "cowardly". Quite clearly our Lord God sees cowardice as being a mark of rebellion against him and something so disgusting that it is a mark of spiritual death and deserves nothing but judgement.

As I was mulling this over I was provoked in my spirit. To what extent is my reluctance to stand resolutely on the Word of God and engage in spiritual warfare through the use of the gifts of the Spirit an expression of cowardice? What *is* cowardice in this sense?

Jesus used the word when confronting the disciples about their lack of faith. The setting was the Sea of Galilee on the occasion when he stilled the storm. He stood in the boat, rebuked the demonic powers driving that particular storm and then said to the Twelve, *"Why are you so afraid? Do you still have no faith?"* (*Matthew 8:26* and *Mark 4:40*)

The normal word for "be afraid" is the verb *PHOBEO*. The word translated "afraid" here however, is the Greek *DEILOS*, which means "cowardly". It appears only three times in the New Testament. It is a very strong term.

Faith in the storm

In *Mark 4:40* and in the equivalent passage in *Matthew 8:26*, the contrast is between cowardice and *faith.* Our Lord stated his purpose for going to the far side of the Sea of Galilee (*35*). He knew his Father had set up a divine appointment for him with Legion, a demonised man from one of the Decapolis towns on the eastern side of the lake. Having told the disciples what was to happen, Jesus settled himself in the stern of the boat (probably lying on folded nets stored under the large shelf located there) and went to sleep on a cushion. This carefree action and his simple, positive statement should have been enough to assure the disciples that come what may they *would* get to the far side of the lake! After all, Jesus had said that's how it would be, so that's how it would be!

Faith is acting upon what the word of God says in spite of adverse circumstances. The word of Jesus should always be good enough as far as we disciples are concerned. When challenged by the enemy, we should cling fast to the word of the Lord and not allow cowardice to deflect us.

There is little doubt that the storm had a demonic quality to it. After all, Jesus, when woken up, stood and *rebuked* the storm. That personalises it. You do not tell weather systems to "Stop it!" They tend not to take too much notice! You tell personalities to "Stop it!" because personalities can hear you. There was clearly a demonic personality behind this storm. It was clearly an opportunity for the disciples to stand fast and be secure in the assuring word Jesus had spoken. Instead, they screamed in their cowardice, *"Don't you care if we drown?"* The disappointment shown by Jesus when he was roused is obvious. And he let it be known. First he dealt with the storm by rebuking it: thereby demonstrating that the authorities of hell could not resist his word of command. The impact was immediate. The wind died down and the raging waters were calmed. It was clearly a miracle, although some sceptics think it merely a coincidence!

I recall an episode on one of my Israel tours. We were staying right on the shore of the lake and had enjoyed an hour's fellowship, soaking up the tranquillity of the scene. During dinner a squall blew up. When we left the dining room we saw the trees bending right over beneath the strength of the wind: the water was rapidly becoming a force to be reckoned with: waves pounding up the beach towards our chalets. The storm raged for several hours. By morning it had abated and we went to breakfast with stillness restored. But the waves were still pounding up the beach. No wind, but still a considerable swell. In the natural there is a delayed reaction in the water under such conditions. Both Matthew and Mark tell us that when Jesus spoke the word to that particular storm, there was immediate calm: both in wind and wave. That made it a miracle.

Trained to do what Jesus would do
The episode suggests that the basis for our Lord's stern rebuke (no pun intended) is that they could have stilled the storm themselves if only cowardice had not got the better of them and led them to undervalue the stated intention of Jesus

(to go to the other side) and the authority he had given to
them.

In *Mark 3:15*, we are told that even at that early stage Jesus
gave his disciples authority to drive out demons. The storm on
the lake occurred *after* that when the disciple training
programme of Jesus was well under way. The disciples should
have learned. They had not and Jesus was disappointed at
their cowardice and impotency in the face of the enemy.

Responding to the challenge
This is very challenging to those of us who have ambitions on
waging war against Satan's kingdom. When we are faced with
the choice between obeying the command of God and
retreating from it, the temptation to cowardice is strong.

The answer to cowardice is robust faith. Do I believe the
confession of God's word has power to deal with the enemy?
Do I trust in the gifts of the Holy Spirit to enable me to
plunder Satan's Kingdom? Our Lord invested heavily in
training the disciples, but his expectation was that they would
apply it practically when confronted, and to do it with
tremendous courage and confidence.

The expectation of Jesus is surprisingly high
It may shock us that Jesus should take such a strong line with
the disciples. We could wish that he showed greater sympathy
with their failure. Perhaps this is down to our settling for a
low faith threshold.

I am seeking to train a group of friends in principles of discipleship. I have been laying great stress on memorising parts of the Bible. *Psalm 119:11* states, *"I have hidden your word in my heart that I might not sin against you."*

I can only hide it in my heart if I have hidden it in my mind first of all. If it is in my memory it can then be hidden in my heart. Not unless. The Psalm says that if I long to be righteous, my strategy must be to hide God's word in my heart.

Part of my training programme is to provide passages of Scripture to memorise. The trainees have a month to remember up to eight or nine verses. Most have kept at it and done it faithfully and in so doing have been completely amazed at the blessing it is to them. Because it is in their memory, they are able to feed on it during the day and even during the night when they wake up with troublesome thoughts. They are beginning to love God's word.

Having said this, one or two have approached me to say they find it hard to memorise Scripture, so can I please let them off! Because they are my friends, everything in me wants to say, "Yes, of course! You surely didn't expect me to insist on it!" But I know I dare not say that. This is critically important. Our Lord overcame Satan in the Wilderness by confessing Scripture that he *knew.* Can we expect it to be any different for us?

Feeding on food requires us to have it in our mouths to start with! The illustration is apt. When Scripture fills my mind, it enables me to meditate on it. It transforms me and provides me with ammunition when I'm attacked. Confessing the word of God has power over Satan.

There on the Sea of Galilee the expectation of Jesus was startlingly high. It has not diminished.

Food for thought … and time for action. Here's hoping!

Chapter Five

Why should I be accountable?

Surprise attack in battle zones demands unrelenting watchfulness. It is no different for those engaged in *spiritual* warfare!

When Jesus spoke to Peter and the apostles concerning the foundation and function of his Church (*Matthew 16:18*), he declared that warfare was its business: attacking Satan's kingdom and successfully defending itself against enemy forces. Throughout his ministry on earth, our Lord showed how to attack and plunder the devil's territory. He used the gifts of the Holy Spirit to heal, deliver, prophesy, bring words of wisdom and knowledge and even raise the dead. In every case, Jesus was attacking Satan's entrenched positions with complete success, setting prisoners free.

When it came to defending himself against the enemy, he used the written Word of God as a sword and the strategy was completely successful. This is our calling too as members of Christ's corporate Body, the Church.

Jesus was in conflict with Satan and with those under Satan's influence. It was Jesus' awareness of Father's promise and the assurance of his Heavenly Home that enabled him to stand strong through the storm (*Hebrews 12:2*).

As they faced coming trouble, Jesus warned the disciples that they must adopt his strategy (*Matthew 5:10-12;10:17-31; John 16:33; etc.*).

Life circumstances
The devil is adept at using the vagaries of life to ambush us. The unexpected catches us off guard and our lack of watchfulness brings about a fall.

We need true discernment to distinguish between spiritual attacks and natural ones. It is common to get them muddled.

We can think something has a natural cause when really it has a cause in the spirit realm. There is a classic example of that distinction in *Mark 4:39*. Who could have supposed that a storm on the Sea of Galilee might have demonic force behind it? Jesus had that level of discernment and it led him to *rebuke* the storm. He told the wind to "Stop it!" It was a clear sign that he knew he was dealing with a personality and not merely a dumb force of nature. Jesus did not *always* deal with storms that way, but in that particular instance he knew it had a satanic source. That's discernment at work.

Conversely we can think something has a spiritual cause when really it has a cause in the natural realm. Some have a tendency to put every conflict down to demonic activity. Instead of repenting of lust and working hard to put it to death, some immediately fly to the excuse, "I must have a *spirit* of lust!" Or in the case of anger, "I need ministry for this *spirit* of anger!" The joy of these excuses is that they remove lust and anger from *my* responsibility and put it squarely on a supposed demonic spirit. "It's down to the *Lord* to release me! It's not *my* fault: you can't blame *me!*"

One great advantage in seeing demons behind my sin and iniquity is that I think it can be dealt with quickly and with little effort. I have a problem: I look for ministry: I get delivered: problem over. Really?

The enemy within
According to the Bible the flesh is a major obstacle to spiritual growth and I am grossly deceived if I fail to recognise it in myself. Passages like *Galatians 5:16-26* should be etched in our consciences and give pause for thought.

Sources of trouble are not only "out there" but are also "in here"! In *Mark 7:20-23* our Lord refers to things that come out of a man and that make him "unclean". The effect of these "evils" is truly destructive to our life of faith and ability to overcome. But these evils are actually *in* us, even though we are Christians. An essential part of our Lord's disciple training is the call to engage the enemy within.

Outward (particularly public) sin is one thing and most of us would consider ourselves to be reasonably controlled as far as that goes: but what about iniquity in the heart? How tight is our personal control as far as that goes? It is easy to think that if we are effective in ministry it must show that we have control over the iniquity in our hearts and that we are doing well. Wrong! It is easy to be deceived right at this point. When our powers of ministry appear undiminished, we can be deluded into thinking we can get away with a low threshold of personal holiness and discipline. Think again!

The history of the Church, both ancient and modern, is littered with casualties – men and women who put success in ministry above personal holiness. The Lord's patience is not inexhaustible! Sooner or later a moment comes when his censure and discipline fall and they often fall publicly.

I tremble (or I *should* tremble) when I read *2 Peter 2.* Peter deals with false teacher-prophets. He exposes them as charlatans; he unwraps their crafty and manipulative public ministry methods; he opens up their inner motives. They will receive their come-uppance at some stage, he says, but not before they have made shipwreck of the faith of many followers not exercising their own discernment. It is a devastating piece of writing and Peter is obviously basing it upon his own observations in the fresh young Church. Believers way back then had many of the same challenges that we have and they had to deal with them in just the same way. Peter's closing words cannot be bettered:

"Therefore, dear friends, since you already know this, be on your guard so that you may not be carried away by the error of lawless men and fall from your secure position. But grow in the grace and knowledge of our Lord and Saviour Jesus Christ. To him be glory both now and for ever! Amen."

"Accountability" – a step too far?

The New Testament lays great emphasis upon devotion to fellowship (*i.e. Acts 2:42*). Close inter-personal relationship was the order of the day and it had practical expression at every level.

Believers did not live in isolation from each other: they shared everything. Transparent openness between them was a definite safeguard.

Teacher-prophets in Peter's day could not have deceived the Lord's people if they had been accountable to brothers who had authority to speak into their lives.

If we are not accountable to our brothers and sisters, we are fair game for the devil's close attention. There are significant numbers of preachers and leaders of the Church who are not accountable to others and so are vulnerable to surprise satanic attack. Some begin to peddle doctrines that are less than the whole truth, others fall into preferences and practices that are thoroughly inappropriate for men and women of God. Because the inclinations of their minds and hearts are closely guarded secrets, nobody knows ... until it is too late.

When a person's ministry elevates him in people's opinions he can so easily be placed beyond challenge. After all, who is of sufficient spiritual stature to challenge such a 'Special One'? Sadly, it is not only admirers who fall into the trap: it can be the adulated minister himself. He may think that his erudition in the pulpit (for instance) places him in a class apart from those in the pew. If he has a television profile or acclaimed writing and speaking ministry the problem may well increase. Who will dare to question him?

A statement found in *1 Samuel 24:6* is sometimes quoted to justify leaving pastors and preachers unchallenged. *"Touch not the Lord's anointed" (Authorised Version)*. This was said by David, Israel's King-in-waiting when he was presented with the opportunity of taking advantage of King Saul. Saul was certainly 'God's anointed' BUT *Kings of Israel are not types of modern Church Ministers. The godly kings are types of King Jesus.* So to use *1 Samuel 24:6* as a prohibition against the challenging of Ministers is very dangerous. We are foolish if we make the mistake of placing preachers, pastors and prophets above normal members of the Body of Christ. When it comes to status in the Church of Jesus Christ we are all members one of another. Hierarchies are features of religion and have no place in the true *EKKLESIA* of Jesus. Of course there are varieties of ministry in the Body of Christ, and some gifted members have particular impact and influence and should be honoured. *But that does not place them beyond challenge and correction.*

Accountability is vital for all of us. We are to submit to each other and care about each other to the extent that we are willing to speak the truth in love. Sometimes the truth hurts: but when it is bathed in love the hurt is soothed and health can be restored. Lindy and I are deeply grateful for men and women to whom we open ourselves and who love us enough to correct us and hold us to account when it is necessary. It's certainly costly discipleship, but it's the only kind I find in the Bible.

Chapter Six

Training really does matter

Success in warfare depends upon many things including the quality of our training. Effective soldiers are prepared to take orders and follow their senior officer on the basis that they know him, they have seen him operate. They trust him and are ready to follow, even when he leads them 'over the top'.

Being 'Church' is like that. Our Lord said *"I will build my Church and the authorities of hell will not be able to overcome it (or to withstand it!)" (Matthew 16:18).* The Greek means both.

It is an extraordinary and encouraging statement, particularly in regard to these End Days when we know from the Scriptures that the true Church will face perilous times before the Lord comes for us. We need training if we are to stand firm under attack and be successful in releasing captives from Satan's kingdom.

The continual emphasis in the training school of Jesus was discipleship. He trained the disciples rigorously and at times scared them so much that many left him (see *John 6:66*). That is the test: when the going gets tough it reveals those who are truly the Lord's disciples and those who are simply nominal.

.

With a relatively tiny number Jesus was able to establish his Church, which he himself described as being capable of defeating Satan's forces and defending itself against them. Warfare is regular service for all in the Church Jesus builds.

The heart of Jesus' Discipleship Training Programme

Three years with Jesus was time well spent! Our Lord was determined to train his disciples and to train them thoroughly. There are various clues to how he did this: the core element was opening up their understanding of the Hebrew Scriptures and showing how to apply them to their personal life and ministry.

In *Luke 24:27* we have the encounter between the risen Jesus and two disciples as they were making their way home from Jerusalem to Emmaus.

*"And beginning with Moses and all the Prophets, he explained to them what was said in **all the Scriptures** concerning himself."*

A few hours later, when they were back in Jerusalem, Jesus appeared to these two once more. But this time in company with the Eleven. *Luke 24:44-49* describes the event. Jesus was soon to ascend and was passing on his final strategic encouragement to the disciples.

*"These are the words I spoke to you **while I was still with you**: everything must be fulfilled that is written about me in the Law of Moses, the Prophets and the Psalms."*

throughout the forty days following his resurrection Jesus was with the disciples for much of the time.

Our Lord spoke of the way all of the Hebrew Scriptures (the Old Testament) pointed to him; our Lord's training was certainly comprehensive! The revelation of Jesus in the Hebrew Scriptures, though startling and revolutionary to Jewish minds, would be fundamental to the success of his Church's mission.

On the same occasion Luke says he *"opened their minds so they could understand the Scriptures" (Luke 24:45)*. The Hebrew Bible is packed with prophetic revelation of Jesus but the understanding of that wonderful truth does not come naturally. According to *John 20:22* it was necessary for our Lord to breathe the Holy Spirit into the disciples: it was the moment of their new birth.

Luke tells us that while still with them, Jesus reinforced his affirmation of the Old Testament,
"This is what is written: Messiah will suffer and rise from the dead on the third day, and repentance and forgiveness of sins will be preached in his name to all nations, beginning at Jerusalem ... " (Luke 24:46-47).

Please note the words, *"This is what is written"*. It is easy to skate over the statement and miss the startling implication in it. Jesus is saying that his suffering and resurrection on the third day are plainly written about in all three sections of the Hebrew Scriptures! Scholars identify hundreds of clear prophetic references and allusions to the crucifixion and resurrection of the Messiah, quite apart from the many other prophetic statements concerning our Lord's person, his life and his ministry!

The ability to understand the revelation of Jesus in the Old Testament came with the new birth, but the disciples would still need to apply themselves to studying the Scriptures in order to discover the treasures of that revelation. It does not come to us 'out of the blue'. The Holy Spirit rewards those who *diligently seek Jesus (Hebrews 11:6).*

The gospel in the Hebrew Scriptures
While it is perfectly plain that we present-day disciples must 'devour' the New Testament, we cannot over emphasize the need to learn, mark and inwardly digest the Hebrew Scriptures as well. They were, after all, the authority that lay behind the gospel preaching of Peter, John, Paul, Philip and all the rest of those early preachers. Indeed, for the first several decades of the Church's existence, there was not a single word of the New Testament! The preaching of the apostles and their associates was based upon the Hebrew Scriptures. In this they took their cue from Jesus himself!

On his own admission, our Lord only ever did what the Father told him to do: he only ever said what the Father gave him to say (see *John 8:28-29*). So a thorough understanding of the whole Word of God will be required if we are truly to discern what Father wants us to say or do.

In *Acts 9:22* we have a fascinating description of Paul's first preaching of the gospel in Damascus.

"Saul grew more and more powerful and baffled the Jews living in Damascus by **drawing together the proofs** *that Jesus is the Messiah."*

I understand from linguistic experts that the phrase *"drawing together the proofs"* is a better rendering of Luke's Greek than the word *"proving"*, as it is rendered in (for instance) the NIV. It shows Paul's method of evangelism as gathering the prophetic statements from the Hebrew Scriptures as the foundation of his gospel proclamation! Exciting, isn't it? When you think about it, it would have to be that way. A Jewish audience would take no notice unless everything was anchored in their own Scriptures. I can imagine Paul sitting among the Damascus Jews and under inspiration of the Holy Spirit teasing out statement after statement that had so recently been veiled to him, but had now become gloriously, splendidly unveiled to reveal Messiah Jesus!

Kingdom Authority

The word Messiah means 'anointed'. In Bible times they anointed priests and kings, so the title declares that Jesus is 'Great High Priest and King of Kings'!

Jesus trained his disciples as a Jewish father would train his son. Sons followed their father's trade and were apprenticed for four years, between the age of thirteen and seventeen. A good tradesman looked to produce a son that would remind people of him: like father, like son! The quality of the son's work and character closely resembled that of his father.

It was customary for such apprentices to spend part of their working day at the *Bet Midrash*, a 'senior school' attached to the synagogue, in which they continued their studies in the Scriptures. A kind of 'sandwich scheme' operated!

At the age of seventeen, a young man chose either to leave the *Bet Midrash* to continue in his father's profession as a qualified tradesman or else he went up to Jerusalem to study the Law under a respected Rabbi. This was the chosen career path followed by Paul (see *Acts 22:3*), but there is no record that Jesus did that. On the contrary, it appears that he continued in his earthly father's business – building and woodworking – until he was thirty. That, after all, is when he began his ministry (*Luke 3:23*).

Of his three years of ministry, Jesus invested a great deal of it in discipling his 'apprentices' (Heb: *TALMIDIM*): much of it demonstrating *how to be like him and to do everything as he would do it.* That was the end in view.

A major demonstration of this is found in our Lord's extended teaching seminar we know as 'The Sermon on the Mount'. Living under the governance of Jesus is to express true Kingdom life. That is what *Matthew 5 – 7* is all about.

Much of the teaching of Jesus is very attractive to the modern mind. The Sermon on the Mount is popular among thinking people. If everyone lived by these great truths, they argue, the world would be a far better place. Even Moslems and Hindus recognise Jesus as a wonderful teacher, *but we must beware of placing our Lord as Teacher first instead of Saviour.* This is a dangerous tendency. The inescapable fact is that if I do not know Jesus the Messiah as my Saviour, I am not capable of applying his kingdom teaching. Only disciples can live as disciples. But so to live is an indispensable part of successful spiritual warfare.

Chapter Seven

Tradition ...tradition!

From time to time (more frequently than I like to admit) I get quite despondent over the level of my devotion to the Lord. It is partly down to the accusations of the devil ... but only partly. At times my discipleship drifts so far away from what the Bible tells me it should be that to compare the two is like chalk and cheese, and I jolly well need to repent and pull myself together.

On such occasions I am amazed that my Father can still be gracious enough to use me in ministry. A letter comes, a remark is made, and people say how blessed they have been through something I have preached or written and it astounds me. How can it be so? If this person knew the true state of my discipleship, he would not be so forthright in his praise.

My question is this: how much *more* could the Lord use me if only I lived the Bible way?

What holds true for individual believers holds true for churches. How much more might they experience the power of heaven let loose if they conformed to *biblical* ways of doing things instead of other ways?

I was sitting in a church the other day, taking part in one of the regular services, when a thought struck me. How recognisable would all this be to a believer transported from the days of the New Testament?

I'm bound to admit that rather naughtily I began drifting off from what was happening in the service and found myself reading *Matthew 15*.

A monstrous delusion
Some Gospel passages crackle with tension. *Matthew 15* is a good example. We find Jesus in open conflict with the Pharisees and teachers of the law. The issue at stake is tradition.

"Why do your disciples break the tradition of the elders?" asked the Jewish leaders.
"And why do you break the command of God for the sake of your tradition?" replied the Lord.

Here Jesus is attacking a terrible 'monster' that had grown insidiously through the centuries since the return of the Jews from exile in Babylon. The religious leaders had breathed life into this destructive monster that was known as "the tradition of the elders".

It came about innocently enough. While in Babylon under captivity, the Jewish elders concluded that their predicament was the direct consequence of breaking God's Law: the Torah given to Israel through Moses. The people were suffering just punishment for their disobedience. Simple!

The question the elders asked was straightforward enough. Let's put it like this:

"Supposing YHWH in His great mercy permitted us to return from Babylon to Judea, what measures might we take to ensure that our people would not fall into disobedience and be sentenced to further captivity? How might we avoid yet more disaster by helping the people not to break God's written Law?"

The answer found was to create a whole new level of prohibitions – extensions of the Mosaic Laws – intended to surround them rather like a protective wall. If the people were observant to keep these lesser prohibitions, there would be no danger of them violating God's Holy Law.

So, for instance, the simple injunction in the Mosaic Law to keep the Sabbath Day holy was walled around with 1500 man-made laws. Be sure to keep those and there would be no danger of disobeying God's *actual* commandment regarding the Sabbath.

To begin with it was made abundantly clear to the people that the traditions of the elders were just that: man-made and not of divine origin. They were intended to *help* the Jews to obey God's Word.

But in the 400 years between the post-exilic return to Judea and the days of Jesus these traditions of the elders had taken on a status equal to the Torah. Leading Rabbis made extraordinary statements such as the following ones quoted in the *Mishnah*:

"It is more punishable to act against the words of the Scribes than those of the Scriptures".
(Tractates Berachot 3:2; Sanhedrin 11:3; Yevamot 89b-90a)

"Give more heed to the words of the Rabbis than to the words of the Law." (Tractate Eravin 21b)

No wonder Jesus confronted the Jewish Hierarchy as he did! *"Why do you break the command of God for the sake of your tradition?"*

Here is proof that some of the traditions of the elders were in stark contrast with the Scriptures. Incredibly, when faced with that contrast, the religious leaders opted for the former. Tradition was placed above the Word of God. Jesus loathed that position and quite deliberately did everything he could to confront it.

The monster lives!
Throughout the history of the Church, faithful believers have sought to slay the monster. It has reared its ugly head at every opportunity, seeking to control the Church and to keep it from functioning as it should. The degree of deception among many believers today is pretty scary and it appears to be increasing. Intellect and denominationalism are placed above Scripture in so many situations: some you would never expect. Churches are prevented from establishing biblical

ways of operating because denominational tradition says, "NO! We do it *this* way!"

One interesting exercise we could try is to read the Book of Acts and the Epistles with an open mind, leaving aside all preconceptions and traditions, and write up an account of what we discover about the life of the Church. What was it like? How did it function?

We could then make a direct comparison between that Church and the one we belong to. Would it be the same? If not, why not? Some distinctives could perhaps be put down to our living at a different time and certain changes due to culture might be permissable ... but what of all the rest?

Such an exercise would be viewed by some as extremely dangerous and very threatening. Why? Are we afraid to discover what a biblical Church looks like?

The same approach might be taken in regard to personal faith. How much of what I believe is directly founded upon the Bible and how much on the traditions of the elders: the doctrines that denominational history has come up with?

Slaying the monster
Disciples of Jesus follow him and learn from him. If *Matthew 15* is anything to go by (and it *is*!) it's about time we rounded on the monster of tradition and slaughtered it, even if it means hacking at it bit by bit.

The battle cry of the Reformation was *"Sola scriptura* (by Scripture alone); *Sola fide* (by Faith alone); *Sola Gratia* (by Grace alone); *Solus Christus* (through Christ alone); *Soli Deo Gloria* (Glory to God alone)". We need to revisit this.

In insisting upon "by Scripture alone" we do not undermine everything associated with organised Churches, but everything associated with organised Churches must yield to the plain teaching of the Bible. We should never give way to the traditions of the elders when they contradict the written Word of God. If there is an obvious clash, there is an obvious adjustment to be made: human tradition, whether ancient or modern, needs to yield to the Word of God - the Sword of the Spirit.

Prepare the Way
When Jesus prepared the disciples for the End Days, he spoke very readily about deception. *Matthew 24* is stuffed with warnings about it. Believers are deceived when they believe they are doing right but are, in truth, doing wrong.

Many people who claim to be Christian are content to live under the dominance of denominational tradition, not seeing its power to divert from Bible truth and thereby become a substitute authority. Challenging it from within can be a costly business in terms of friendship and fellowship. All too easily we can be dismissed as 'boat rockers', legalists and those lacking in love.

The tragedy is that Christians and churches electing to follow human tradition rather than the Scriptures cannot possibly know what they are missing in terms of personal growth and corporate power. Comparing ourselves with Christians and Churches described in the New Testament provides powerful contrast and powerful clues.

The Lord is *so* merciful to us. He favours Christians with his blessing and allows us to serve him through ministry, *but how much **more** might he use us if only we would turn from tradition and return to the Word?*

What now?
Time was when I was a reasonable Organist. I loved playing the works of Bach. One of his cantatas includes the chorale *"Wachet auf, ruft uns die Stimme"*. A rough translation is, "Wake up *now* – the night is flying!"

I reckon that is what the Lord is saying to his Church right now. Our wonderful Messiah is soon returning and night will become glorious day! But it is vital that we *wake up* and wake up **now**!

We need to give each other a good shake to jolt us out of our slumbers. The Lord is urgently shouting, "Wake up! Wake up! Wake up! Get out of your comfort zone and get back to my Word."

Well …?

54

Chapter Eight

Living by the Word

When Joshua led the people of Israel through the Jordan he was a man on a mission. The Lord had called him to an extremely demanding ministry: taking on where the great Moses had left off.

It was a case of "Follow that!" and some of us know a little of the pressure Joshua must have been under. When we take on a work after an illustrious predecessor has left it, it is not long before comparisons are made. "Moses never did it *this* way!"

Battle strategy in Canaan
The challenge for Joshua must have been enormous. How to cope? Obviously the right strategy was not to try to walk in a dead man's sandals because they simply would not fit! Joshua would need to be his own man … or more correctly, the man *God* wanted him to be. The degree to which Joshua followed the tradition of Moses was only the degree to which it conformed to the Word delivered by the Lord *through* Moses at Sinai.

Joshua was called by the Lord and he walked in that calling without turning to the right or the left. I am always hugely impressed with the way he responded to the forthright command and promise of the Lord recorded in *Joshua 1:6-9.*

"Be strong and courageous, because you will lead these people to inherit the land I sword to their forefathers to give them. Be strong and very courageous. Be careful to obey all the law my servant Moses gave you; do not turn from it to the right or the left, that you may be successful wherever you go. Do not let this Book of the Law depart from your mouth; meditate on it day and night, so that you may be careful to do everything that is written in it. Then you will be prosperous and successful. Have I not commanded you? Be strong and courageous. Do not be terrified; do not be discouraged, for the Lord your God will be with you wherever you go."

And that is just what Joshua did. His life reflected his calling perfectly. One thing motivated him: the Word of God as delivered at Sinai: what we call the Torah (Pentateuch).

The Truth, the whole Truth and nothing but the Truth
I do not doubt that Moses and Joshua had spent precious hours in matchless fellowship together and that Moses had passed on many insights gleaned from his eighty years experience, but as far as God was concerned just one thing was needful: the Book of the Law. God's written Word.

Note the command, *"Do not let this Book of the Law depart from your **mouth; meditate** on it day and night"?* It was to be Joshua's constant activity, both waking and sleeping! What does that mean? It means Joshua needed to teach God's Word continually. He was required to keep it in his mouth all the time, ministering the written Word as a constant activity. It is reminiscent of *Malachi 2*, where we find the Lord describing the true priesthood of Levi.

Here are verses 5-7, *"... he revered me and stood in awe of my name. True instruction was in his mouth and nothing false was found on his lips. He walked with me in peace and uprightness, and turned many from sin. For the lips of a priest ought to preserve knowledge, and from his mouth men should seek instruction – because he is the messenger of the Lord Almighty."*

When people heard Levi and Joshua they were perfectly aware that they were listening to the pure written Word of God infused with the prophetic power of the Holy Spirit. Here was their authority, the secret of their leadership.

Malachi was a post-exilic prophet. By his day the Torah had suffered at the hands of well intentioned religious leaders who had corrupted the written Word by supplementing it with the traditions of the elders. With the passage of time, these supplements took on such elevated status that God's people were encouraged to live by the traditions of their elders even when they violated the written Word. How different from the command of the Lord delivered to Joshua, for whom success and victory were dependent upon his mouth speaking out *only* what was stated in the Book of the Law. In the words of the Reformation, *"Sola Scriptura!"*

Where the rubber hits the road
The deceptive tricks of the devil do not vary enormously through the passage of history. They always seem to work well whether we're considering his manipulation of Israel or the Church. Take the matter of 'the tradition of the elders'. That monster is very much alive and well today.

It is the devilish tendency to place *our* way of doing things above the *Bible* way of doing things and considering it good and right.

I am getting pretty cute at spotting it in its more obvious manifestations, but it works at subtle levels as well. How often do I attend the Lord's Supper without addressing the bad relationship I have with a fellow believer? Do I think it doesn't matter? If I choose to ignore the biblical injunctions governing the Lord's Supper have I not treated the Lord's Supper as a mere religious observance? I am quick to accuse certain people attending Confessionals of being hypocrites, spilling the beans in the box and then going out and sinning all over again, but what of the hypocrisy I display at the Lord's Table from time to time? God's Word is crystal clear on the matter. Read all about it in *1 Corinthians 11:17ff* and compare *Matthew 5:23-24*.

The denominational spirit has become very strong in certain sections of the Church. I know of Charismatic churches where members are so controlled by priestcraft that they are fed the line, *"Leave this fellowship and you leave God behind."* Is that cultic fear less terrible than the Roman Catholic maxim, *"extra Ecclesiam nulla salus"* – "No salvation outside the (Roman) Church"?

The traditions of the elders are killers. They destroy biblical faith and practice. Small wonder that the apostle Peter was so forthright in his condemnation of them in *1 Peter 2:8*.

"See to it that no-one takes you captive through hollow and

*deceptive philosophy, which depends on human tradition and
the basic principles of this world rather than on Christ.*"

That's pretty plain isn't it?

Bible knowledge is not enough
Joshua was instructed to *meditate* on God's written Word day
and night. That means, all the time. If Joshua was not
meditating in the Word himself, how could he expect to speak
the Word into the lives of the people?

I am told that the word 'meditate' has links in Hebrew to the
word, 'ruminate'. A ruminant (like a cow) takes food into its
mouth, chews in thoroughly, swallows it and then brings it up
again to chew it yet more. It repeats the operation several
times before swallowing it for good! This process extracts
every bit of nutrition from the 'green stuff' before it is
digested.

How suggestive! Have you noticed how a recumbent cow is
always chewing? That's because it knows what's good for it!

In giving Joshua his battle strategy, the Lord instructed him to
meditate in the Word day and night. Not only was he to 'chew
it over', to extract every scrap of revelation it could have for
him, but he was also required to swallow it: to digest it so that
it could become part of him and build him up: to *change* him!

And notice how this was to happen not only in the waking
hours of daytime but also at night, when he was sleeping.

When my mind is filled with God's written Word and I have been 'chewing it over' all day long it goes with me into my sleep and continues to minister to me all night long. Have you noticed how you sometimes wake in the night with God's Word in your mind? That demonstrates this principle at work. Hallelujah!

It is important to recognise that a cow cannot chew what it does not have in its mouth. Similarly you and I cannot meditate upon Scripture we have not read (better still, memorised). Bible study is critically important for our survival.

Equally, if a cow refuses to chew the cud and, biting off a bunch of grass, simply spits it straight out again, that grass, though full of nutrition, will have no impact in the cow's body and the cow will become useless.

Same for me!

Am I 'into Bible study' or am I being changed by the Word? Christians are very keen on Bible study. They will travel many miles to hear a good Bible teacher. They buy CDs and DVDs as well as books in the sure knowledge that knowing the Bible is vital. It is. But without receiving the revelation and allowing it to change us we are missing the point. We can so easily end up grossly obese, having stuffed ourselves with Bible knowledge, when the need is to be fit for action. *That spiritual food has got to be digested.*

This is one of God's Government health warnings!

Chapter Nine

On with the running shoes!

The New Testament books were written at a time when genuine churches were under threat from the Roman authorities and from Rabbinic Judaism. Added to this opposition was the real and present danger from demonic religions deeply entrenched in the Roman world. Strong reactions to the gospel were guaranteed.

The Early Church had also to contend with profound threats from within: the opposition of false teachers and those who were their devotees. From the very start Christians determined to live biblically faced tremendous challenges.

Trouble in store?
In response, the New Testament writers wrote with trouble in mind. They acknowledged that peaceful co-existence with the enemies of Jesus Christ was never an option. To be a disciple of Jesus meant warfare all the way and those for whom the writers wrote needed to be encouraged ... and *trained to fight with spiritual weapons.*

Whilst it was tough for Gentile believers, Jewish Christians had a particularly hard time of it. When baptised they faced banishment from both synagogue and family. In extreme Orthodox families a convert to Christ was counted as dead.

If married, his wife was snatched away from him and taken back into her family fold. She was even free to marry again because her Christian husband was counted dead and so she was treated as a widow.

Keeping faith under wraps

Trouble might be avoided if a Jewish convert was a *secret* believer: giving the impression of still maintaining the Jewish faith while worshipping Jesus privately as an individual.

Though attractive in a hostile environment, keeping quiet about being a Christian was never possible for those with a genuine love for Christ. It was vital that Jewish believers should be built up and encouraged to stand firm and to function as the Body of Christ. Deciding to follow Jesus really did mean there could be no turning back and many had made that level of commitment at great personal cost ... but there was always a temptation to recant.

Avoiding the slippery slope

The Letter to the Hebrews was written to encourage Jewish believers not to snuggle back under the cover of Judaism. The first part of the letter gloriously declares the supremacy of Jesus over everything associated with the Old Hebrew Covenant. Jesus, the divine Son, is the radiance of God's glory and exact representation of His person (*1:3*); Jesus is utterly superior to the angels (*1:4 ff*); He is greater than Moses (*3:3*); Jesus is the Great High Priest in the order of Melchidzedek (*4:14, 5:7-10, 7:27-28*); Jesus is the High Priest of a better Covenant than the old one (*9:11-15*); Jesus has become a single sacrifice that makes all others obsolete (*9:23-28, 10:11-14*).

We cannot be sure who the unnamed writer was: but his grasp of the glorious truth concerning the supremacy of Jesus is stupendous. Having built such an extraordinary case for Christ, he launches into a wonderful exhortation to hold on to our faith and never to waver (*10:19ff*).

In *Hebrews 11* the writer presents his readers with a remarkable cavalcade of the faithful from the Old Testament time. His purpose is clear: he urges his readers to be like these heroes and heroines in their resolution to stand firm whatever the level of provocation.

On with the running shoes!
Hebrews 12:1-12 urges true devotion to Jesus: running the race of faith and submitting to God's discipline, without which the race will not be won.

"Since we are surrounded by such a great cloud of witnesses ..." Verse 1 links us with the heroes of faith recently mentioned. They are referred to as a *cloud* of witnesses. A curious description. Perhaps the word should be *crowd*? But, no, there is no printing error (!), the word *cloud* is used. What is meant?

The writer has in mind a Roman stadium in which an athletics meeting is in progress. Runners are lined up ready to run as if their lives depended upon it. The terraces are packed with witnesses – the spectators.

As the runners hurtle down the track, focused on the finishing line, they are well aware of the shrieking crowds but due to their focus on the finishing line the crowds appear hazy to them: they are immensely encouraged to run their hearts out but their focus is on their goal.

This is such a wonderful picture. We are utterly focused on Jesus and nothing will deflect us: but oh how gloriously encouraging it is when we "sense" the approval and thunderous applause of the faithful saints in the Scriptures. Their testimonies inspire us to great exploits!

"Let us throw off everything that hinders ..."
The Greek word *ONKON* means excess weight. Slimmers know all about it (!) and so do athletes. No excess weight can be carried if we have aspirations to be successful. Excess weight is internal – it lies under the surface. In the context of running the faith race it refers to those areas of weakness that are inward: part of us, for which we make excuses. Rather like an obese person who excuses his condition as glandular or as being the result of having heavy bones!

We are speaking of iniquity in the heart: pride, lust, resentment, greed, criticism, anger, bitterness and so forth. These are not outwardly obvious, they lie under the surface, but their effect on our outward actions is devastating. These are the driving forces that lead us to commit outward sin. In *Matthew 5* our Lord referred to anger as being the driving force leading to murder (*5:21-22*) and lust as leading to adultery (*5:27-28*). So quite plainly if I keep anger and lust under control I will never run the risk of murdering anyone.

Lindy will never have cause to weep because I have been unfaithful to her if I am in control of lust in my life.

The lusts of the flesh are devastating in their effect and it is the wise disciple that deals with them ruthlessly.

"and the sin that so easily entangles ... "
Here the writer to the Hebrews speaks of *external* hindrances that prevent us from running. Imagine setting off down the track in a Roman toga! You wouldn't get far before falling flat on your nose and becoming a laughing stock.

In the Roman Games, runners were naked. Jews would never take part or even attend because of it (and also because the athletes were required to dedicate themselves to Roman gods in pre-race rituals). But although our writer never attended, he would have been well aware of what went on in the stadium.

The picture of the runner with no clothing whatsoever is pertinent. In the writer's mind is the absolute requirement to cast off *everything* that hinders progress. Make your own list! How many "things" do you consider essential to life which are completely superfluous? What relationships have you that hinder your faith? What activities do you engage in that are counterproductive to active faith?

Training for spiritual warfare requires this kind of discipline. If we are to run the race with perseverance, demonstrating our commitment to Jesus, these are issues we cannot overlook.

"Let us run with perseverance the race marked out for us ... "

While it is plain that we each have our own life course to run along, it is surely true that we are required to run by faith in the same way as other disciples. There is a predetermined course that all disciples of Jesus have followed. And always will. That is why we are able to encourage each other and why we must *do* so. It is the reason why the heroes in the stands are able to encourage as they do: they have run the very same course. They learned the track, they negotiated the stumbling blocks and the slippery sections. Their experience is written up in the Hebrew Scriptures and we benefit from it … if we have any sense.

"Let us fix our eyes on Jesus, the pioneer and perfecter of our faith …"
Never take your eyes off the Lord! Our faith starts and finishes with Him! Jesus is the source of our faith and He is the goal of our faith. This is a very practical matter. The Bible frequently reveals that where true believers are facing terrible suffering they are provided with revelation of Jesus. Stephen is a fine example. Acts 7:54ff shows clearly that as Stephen was about to be smashed to mortar by the great boulders hurled down on him by his murderers, he saw heaven opened and Jesus standing at the right hand of the Father. That joy set before him inspired and strengthened him to endure the torture.

Isn't it astonishing to observe that this is precisely the pattern shown in the experience of our Lord Himself? *Read Hebrews 12:2* and be massively encouraged. The joy of re-entering His heavenly home and the satisfaction of knowing what His death would accomplish strengthened our dear Saviour to endure the cross.

As we contemplate the glorious person of Jesus and the promise of our eternal security, we are able to face the fiercest trial. That is a great secret of our warfare. It is the stuff of discipleship.

Lesson Ten

Glory! Glory! Hallelujah!

Just recently I was 'attending' the wedding at Cana in Galilee, observing the terrible social tragedy for that family when the wine ran out (*John 2:1-11*). Mary went to Jesus with the problem and in spite of his testing response, *"Woman, what does your concern have to do with me?"* she went straight to the servants and told them in no uncertain terms, *"Do whatever Jesus tells you."*

In my own experience there are some instances when, having taken a matter to the Lord in prayer, he appears not to respond straight away. How should we react? Mary knew Jesus better than anyone on earth. She knew he had all the necessary power to answer her plea, so she acted as though she had received what she asked for – a miracle. "Do whatever Jesus tells you" was a comment made in faith. It was completely justified! The wine produced was of such quality that the Toast Master was overawed.

Seeing the glory
It is far from the simple story it appears to be at first sight. It serves a mighty purpose that the writer, John, wanted to achieve: the creation and encouragement of faith through the revelation of Jesus and his glory.

The miracle at Cana closes with the words, *"He thus revealed his glory and his disciples put their faith in him"* (*John 2:11*).

It is always helpful to know why Scripture writers wrote. John gives his clear purpose in *John 20:30-31*, where he writes that he has made a personal selection of the miraculous signs Jesus performed *"that you may believe that Jesus is the Messiah, the Son of God, and that by believing you may have life in his name."*

Well, that's clear enough. John is not writing to provide an exhaustive account of Jesus' life and ministry. He is honest enough to admit that he is writing with 'an angle'. His purpose is theological as well as historical. His entire gospel account is solid fact, but John has selected certain miraculous signs because they serve to show that faith came to people who saw what Jesus did, acknowledged that the sign pointed to his messiahship and divinity, and in consequence they put their faith in him.

Seeing the glory and living by faith
You'll discover that pattern in each instance of Jesus performing a miracle in John's account: they are signs pointing to the glory of Jesus and that revelation creates and builds faith.

I am told that the Orthodox Jewish leaders had, during the centuries leading up to the time of Jesus, decided among themselves that certain types of miracle were 'messianic'. They insisted that only the true Messiah would be able to perform such signs.

When a teacher was recognised as a 'wonder-worker', the authorities in Jerusalem were duty bound to check him out. Could this man really be the Messiah? If he was, Rome's nemesis had arrived and Israel's consequent destiny would be glorious!

But would it not be utterly disastrous if Messiah came and his coming went unrecognised? Hence we find the religious authorities coming from Jerusalem to assess the genuineness of Jesus (*Mark 3:22; 7:1*). It was a long and expensive journey from Jerusalem to Galilee, but even so their sense of responsibility meant they were bound to check him out for themselves. They could not risk failing to recognise the Messiah. The restoration of the Kingdom to Israel depended upon it.

Religious leaders lived all around the country, but whoever they were and wherever they lived, the need to decide about Jesus' claim to be Messiah was a priority (*Luke 5:17*). In the gospel accounts the Jewish leaders seem to bob up continually in a determined effort to scrutinise what Jesus said and did: questioning him with the utmost vigour (*Matthew 16:1; 19:3; 22:41-46; Mark 8:11; 10:2; John 7:26; 10:24*).

"There's none so blind ..."
Remarkably, the seven miraculous signs in John's account match the nominated sign-list precisely! But although the authorities were constantly asking Jesus to see miracles, the moment they witnessed one they dismissed it as devilish (*Mark 3:22*)! There is a tragic irony about all this.

In those days there were healings of blind people from time to time, but Jesus healed a man *born* blind (*John 9:32*); there were people raised from the dead (and a number of examples are provided in both the Old and New Testaments) but raising a dead man after three days and nights was completely unheard of until Jesus raised up Lazarus (*John 11:39*). These and the other johannine signs were just what the Rabbis were trained to look for. Tragically, however, they had blinded themselves to the possibility that Jesus of Nazareth was truly the Messiah. As the old adage goes, "The man compelled against his will is of the same opinion still!"

John makes a telling point in John 2:11. "The first of his miraculous signs Jesus performed in Cana of Galilee. He thus revealed his glory and his disciples put their faith in him."

Faith was kindled through seeing the revelation of Christ's *glory*. That's what the miraculous sign accomplished. Amazing though it may seem, the miracle by itself did not create faith: it was beholding the *glory* that did it. Furthermore, nobody else is mentioned as believing: it was only the disciples in this instance.

This suggests that only determined disciples of Jesus are able to see his glory in what he does and therefore exercise faith, and furthermore that revelation of the glory is a divine gift.

The indifferent see the same miracle but react with incredulity, even accusing Jesus of exercising demonic power (*Matthew 12:23-24*)!

A threefold revelation

The creation and building of faith is such a vital element in our relationship with God that while every Bible book has it as a main emphasis, several books are *devoted* to it. The Gospel account of John is one, Hebrews is another. The first part of that mighty letter is devoted to expounding the utter supremacy of Christ over all. However, at *10:19* a dramatic change occurs. The writer introduces the whole matter of *faith* as *response to the revelation of Christ's glory!*

The Letter was written to Jewish Christians who were under great pressure to fall back into the perceived security of Judaism. As devoted disciples of Jesus Christ, they stood to lose family and friends, financial security and be sure of social exile. What a price to pay. Better, surely, to retreat into *secret* discipleship: holding on to an outward Jewish orthodoxy while maintaining faith in Messiah Jesus behind closed doors. It is into that cauldron of socio/religious tribulation that the Letter to the Hebrews was lobbed. How could these people be encouraged to stand fast in the face of such open hostility? Simply by keeping the vision of the glory of Christ in the centre and allowing everything else to sink into the shadows. Here is the same pattern we saw in the Gospel account written by John.

The most obvious book of the Bible that deals with this critical matter is The Revelation of Jesus Christ to John. It is without doubt the most neglected book of the New Testament. Very few Christians read it, let alone study it and feed on it. So it is scarcely surprising that faith is low at the present time and eternal hope is virtually off the radar.

The *main* purpose for which our Father has provided 'Revelation' is not to provide us with eschatological clubs with which to belt the living daylights out of one another. Are we Pre-Trib., Post-Trib., Mid-Trib., A-Millennial, Pre-Millennial, Post-Millennial? Will we be raptured or won't we? If so, when and how? Will we be on the Throne, before the Throne, behind the Throne or even *under* the Throne?

Many of these questions and positions are critically important, that's for sure, but they are not the main purpose for the book! It is plain from the text that the main purpose is *revelation of Jesus Christ (Revelation 1:1; 1:12-18, etc.).* In his own glorious way, the Holy Spirit uses the chapters of the 'Apocalypse' to breathe revelation of the glorified Jesus into us. The result is faith – *real* faith.

Where there's hope there's life!
As the end-time battle grows fiercer and hotter, it is only our eternal hope that will hold us firm in our faith. To be focussed on the glory of Jesus and confident in his ultimate plan for us means we are not earth-bound in our thinking. Is our inappropriate obsession with 'this life' the reason why we grasp for prosperity, recoil from suffering and spend vast sums on health-care and do everything we can to avoid death? If we were abiding in Christ would we not be released from so much that holds us back?

The time has come for us to turn away from fear of the future and resolve to have faith *for* the future. The transition will depend upon the focus of our vision.

Are we focused upon the things of this world and the challenges of the end times or is our focal point the glorious person of Jesus the Messiah: our Great High Priest and King of Kings?

We look to Jesus: the pioneer and perfecter of our faith.

Chapter Eleven

Danger - Crumbling Pillars!

Southwold has a pier. We like Southwold. We like the pier. The pier stands on stanchions that are sunk deep into the seabed so it's perfectly safe to walk right along to the end. Mind you, the North Sea tides swirl constantly around the stanchions and sometimes give them a terrific pounding. The stress and erosion processes have to be watched constantly.

Pillars of society
Our country stands upon a set of stanchions that hold it up. We might include the Monarchy, Parliament, the Church, Law and Order, Armed Forces, Financial Institutions. Then we might add the Media, Health, Education, Commerce and Industry. We could add Morality, Marriage and Family life to the mix. Such are pillars upon which our nation stands. If, at a point in our history, one or two have been weak, others have been strong to take the strain. But imagine a situation in which all the pillars are crumbling away at the same time! What hope is there then?

To be brutally honest, I cannot see a single pillar in our society that is now standing strong. All are crumbling fast. And now that is happening, nothing can hold us up? Our beloved Britain is crumbling away.

Now I admit that such could be described as an intensely negative and pessimistic attitude. But is it accurate?

Pessimism and optimism are both godless attitudes because neither is truth. Sons of God are to be consummate *realists* because that's how God is.

The God who sees
The Lord sees all the affairs of men, not as men would *like* him to see them but exactly as they *are*. God's Word provides us with that perspective.

Bible translation (or *any* translation) is not an exact science. There are sometimes several equally valid ways of translating words and verses. *Psalm 11* contains a good example. The Hebrew of *Ps 11:3* can be translated, *"When the foundations are being destroyed, what is the Righteous One doing?"*

He is allowing the consequences of man's refusal to acknowledge Him to take their natural course. Left to itself, society goes rotten. The Lord is permitting it to happen. It's not His *fault*: He has given fair warning, but our society has chosen to raise two fingers to the Lord and His Word and there are obvious results. *Ps 11:5* says, *"The Lord, the Righteous One, examines the wicked, and those who love violence his soul hates"*. So He is aware of Britain's deliberate rejection of Him and expresses His righteous anger accordingly.

But that statement can be translated just as fairly as *"The Lord examines the righteous ... ."*

If the Lord examines the righteous, what does He see? A very searching question, isn't it? Does it make you feel comfortable or just a teeny bit uneasy?

Ps 11:3 can be translated, *"When the foundations are being destroyed, what can the righteous do?"*

Present indications are that the righteous can do nothing and are content to keep their heads down and to leave it that way! The fear that is mounting through moral collapse, violence and economic strictures appears to impact Christians as well as non believers. So what can the righteous do?

Out of the trench ... over the top!
We are to take up our battle positions and engage with enemy forces - principalities and powers - but to do it the *Lord's* way. How do you feel about creeping out from behind the barricade and taking your stand?

We are called to open warfare with Satan's forces and it can sometimes feel as if our weapons are inferior to his. Enemy forces seem gigantic and totally threatening. The great temptation is to turn and run for it! We frequently suffer defeat because we lack confidence in our God-given weapons and ability to stand. That is the situation addressed by the Lord through *1 Samuel 17*.

David and Goliath
It is surprising that in the Hebrew Bible the history books are classified under 'Prophets'. While the 'Latter Prophets' wrote their prophecies, the 'Former Prophets' did not.

The 'Former Prophets' proclaimed them and lived them in the events recorded in the history books: God has always spoken through their stories. Second to none is the account of David's triumph over Goliath. When I need encouragement to face a major obstacle, the vision of Goliath's massive head bouncing down the hill towards the bottom of the Valley of Elah gives me a real lift!

Being challenged by great odds is part of our calling and we are required to face and overcome them, however daunting the prospect. The secret is to know that even if we have to get involved personally and even suffer in the process, the battle belongs to the Lord.

Scholars tell us that the Philistines originated in the area surrounding the Aegean Sea. When the Greeks began to dominate the area Sea Peoples sought pastures new. When Abraham arrived in Canaan, Philistines already dwelt in Gerar to the south of Gaza and, at that time, they appear to have been reasonable neighbours (see Genesis 20:21 and 26). Things had changed by the time the Israelites were on the march from Egypt and Exodus 13:17 reveals a militant, hostile attitude. In Joshua's day the Philistines occupied five cities along the Gaza Strip (Joshua 13:2-3). The Lord allowed that occupation so that conflict with the Philistines could train Israel for war (Judges 3:1-4). Conflict with the enemy is the Lord's way of building faith into us. Spiritual Warfare is a main element in being the true Church (Matthew 16:18).

The Philistine army moved up from the Coastal Plain and occupied land a few miles west of Bethlehem (1 Sam 17:1).

David was just a teenager at the time and the Philistine expansion threatened David's family, creating fear and insecurity in the community. Significantly there is no mention in the Bible of Israel's government or people seeking God at this time: the whole picture is one of indolence and terror.

Close by the Philistine camp at Socoh lies the Valley of Elah where the battle lines were drawn. Goliath may well have been a descendant of the Anakim or Rephaim, giants who inhabited Canaan when Moses' spies were sent there (*Numbers 13:33*). Joshua destroyed those living in Hebron when Israel entered Canaan and the only survivors lived on Philistine land (*Joshua 11:21-22*).

Goliath was nine feet tall and must have cut a ferocious figure. In his massive armour and with his enormous weapons he was terrifying. When he uttered his challenges, defying the Lord God, the men of Israel shook with fear. How could they take on Goliath on his terms? He knew and understood the score and filled with disdain he spewed out his venomous taunts, believing himself unassailable.

There was actually only one man in the ranks of Israel who came anywhere close to Goliath in physical size, and that was King Saul. *1 Samuel 9:2* says Saul was a head taller than any of his contemporaries, so if there was a single person who might stand any chance against Goliath it was Saul! But Saul had no appetite for the challenge! Consequently there were no challengers. Nobody could challenge Goliath on his stated terms.

It is notable that in spite of incredible miracles of grace that peppered the history of Israel, the King and people no longer considered God to be the centre of the nation's life. Samuel is scarcely mentioned between his visit to Jesse's home to anoint David and Samuel's death (*1 Samuel 16:13* and *25:1*). God's prophet was certainly marginalised in the present conflict: the battle strategy was viewed as the responsibility of King and government. Their natural resources would have to do. But they wouldn't do! The scenario has a contemporary ring.

Fear of the enemy governed God's people. It did not lead them to Him. Consequently government and people were powerless, defeated and filled with shame. But David saved the day. He rejected Saul's armour (*1 Samuel 17:38-39*): it was thoroughly inappropriate for what the Lord wanted to do. It was the obvious requirement for worldly strategy but was useless for killing Goliath.

"I cannot go in these!" This decision was not only vital in order for the Lord to gain the victory through David: it is a vital insight for us as we are confronted with our Goliaths. We are familiar with the jeering ridicule meted out to David by the Philistine champion and troops, but can you imagine the chagrin and downright shame that the Israelites felt at the sight of young David moving down the slope to meet certain death? But David's weaponry allowed maximum scope for the intervention of the Lord. The stone whirled from the sling, it streaked through the air, sunk into Goliath's forehead and crushed his brain.

Some say Goliath died of surprise because such a thing had never entered his head before! I'll tell you one thing – all those drawn up for battle nearly died of surprise! God is the God of surprises. When the Lord takes the field, his faithful servants are the ones who are the true giants! Giants of faith!

As the Psalmist wrote, "May God arise and may his enemies be scattered!" (Psalm 68:1)

Amen and amen!

Chapter Twelve

A Team event

Children in Need is a children's charity that has raised millions of pounds for youngsters in desperate situations. A couple of years ago, one of the fund-raising exploits featured a TV presenter – Matt Baker – who 'pulled' a rickshaw behind a pedal cycle all the way from Scotland to London's BBC Television Centre. It took him a week of gruelling, concentrated effort: completing each daily stage up hill and down dale, resting only when each stage was completed. Matt sometimes cried with the sheer agony he felt in his limbs as he laboured up steep moorland roads. But he was driven on by the goal he had set himself. It was an astonishing achievement.

When speaking of it afterwards Matt said how much he was encouraged to keep going by the thousands of supporters who turned out along the route to cheer him on his way.

It made me think of *Hebrews 12* and the *"great cloud of witnesses"* mentioned. These are the faithful believers whose faithfulness is catalogued in the Hebrew Scriptures. Great men and women of the Old Testament who inspire us by their testimonies and who, across the running centuries, cry out, "Go on! Go on! Go on! You can do it! We did it before you and the Lord will give *you* grace to win through as well!"

I was moved when Matt Baker testified to the special strength he drew from having a close team around him. "Without them I couldn't have done it!" He would never have made it without his trainer and physiotherapist, not to mention producer, cameramen, sound engineers and others too. One member of his team cycled alongside him throughout and stayed there simply to give moral support and keep him focused.

I thought it a wonderful picture of our own *faith* race. The Lord brings encouragement to us at two levels: we have the glorious testimony of biblical saints who encourage us by their example, but we also need the active involvement of living brothers and sisters as we run the race, battling the odds, focused on our goal – our Lord Jesus the Messiah, the pioneer and perfecter of our faith.

I believe it is all too easy for us to neglect the team running with us. The faith race is a team event. We're not competing against one another, we're running as a unit, intent upon driving each other on to achieve our personal goal.

During 2012 we were bombarded with the London Olympics! As summer approached our papers were full of sport and the TV Circus cranked up into full swing. For some of us it was all a bit 'over the top' and I heard of quite a number of Londoners who simply could not face it and planned to be 'out of town' for the duration!

Extreme athleticism was certainly on display and it provoked many of us to 'do something' about our own level of fitness.

And not only our *physical* fitness. I know for me *Hebrews 12:1-2* was reverberating around my head with monotonous regularity and has been ever since!

"Therefore since we are surrounded by such a great cloud of witnesses, let us throw off everything that hinders and the sin that so easily entangles, and let us run with perseverance the race marked out for us. Let us fix our eyes on Jesus, the author and perfecter of our faith …"

If I am not fit to run, I cannot run. That's the hard truth. I do not do it by watching it. I do it by doing it.

And that is where I need the active involvement of brothers and sisters. I need you and you need me. But what I am after is close relationship that actually achieves something. I don't want you on the touchline or in the stand: I want you on the track alongside me!

Those in Matt Baker's Team had *his* success in their sights and they showed a commitment and determination to ensure that he won through come what may. They were with him all the way. This is how the Body of Christ operates … or not, as the case may be.

One of the great statements of the New Testament is James 5:16, "Confess your sins to one another and pray for each other so that you may be healed."

The word *"sins"* may better be translated *"faults"*. Not in the sense of shortcomings, but in the sense of areas of weakness such as in the earth's crust.

The San Andreas Fault is a massive area of structural weakness in the earth's crust that runs through California. It makes that area of the United States particularly vulnerable to seismic pressure.

A gigantic fault runs from Syria, through the Jordan Valley and down to the Great Lakes of Tanzania. It is known as the Syro-African Rift Valley. It traverses the entire land of Israel from north to south and through the running centuries enormous forces have produced earthquakes and volcanic eruptions in the area.

When James writes about faults he means those areas in our lives where we are vulnerable to Satan's forces. It's fighting talk. If I am to run the faith race, to be an overcomer and win the battle, one of the main areas of fitness I need to concentrate heavily on is dealing with the faults that are lurking under my skin. They are not apparent to others, but their *effects* are only too visible. I am aware of my faults: you are not because they are inside me, sometimes visible and at other times, not.

Let me explain.

You cannot see anger, but you can see the *results* of it. You cannot see pride, but you can see its *effect* in me. Our Lord touched on this in the Sermon on the Mount: the Kingdom manifesto for disciples, delivered to those truly committed to Jesus (*Matthew 5:1* and *27* show that whilst crowds were listening in, Jesus was in fact directing his teaching towards the disciples).

Matthew 5:21-22 and *27-28* indicate that murder is an expression of anger, whilst adultery is an expression of lust. Murder and adultery are outward manifestations of anger and lust. Anger and lust are faults of the type referred to by James. If I deal with anger and have control over it, I will never run the risk of murdering someone. If I have the mastery over lust, Lindy need have no fears about me being unfaithful to her.

Other faults might include avarice, conceit, cravings, criticism, bitterness, greed, deceit, envy, rebelliousness and hate. Such are described variously in the Scriptures as
desires of the flesh (*Galatians 5:16* KJV)
sinful desires of the heart (*Romans 1:24*)
evil desires of the mortal body (*Romans 6:12*)
desires of the sinful nature (Romans 13:14; Galatians 5:16 and 2 Peter 2:10)
worldly passions (*Titus 2:12*)
sinful desires that war against your soul (*1 Peter 2:11*)
lust of the flesh, lust of the eyes and the pride of life (*1 John 2:16* KJV)
ungodly desires (*Jude 18*)

James describes the process by which these hidden faults develop and finally burst out with disastrous results. Here is *James 1:14-15*,
"… each one is tempted when, by his own evil desire, he is dragged away and enticed. Then, after desire has conceived, it gives birth to sin; and sin, when it is full-grown, gives birth to death."

When we find a fault in us being stimulated by the enemy, failure to resist it results with it being conceived in me. As I permit it to develop it finally bursts out as sin. Dealing with it at the temptation stage is the guarantee of victory!

The process of discipleship is fraught with serious challenges. The faith race requires hard training and the strong, involved support of a team that is committed to seeing us emerge as champions.

That process requires my willing submission to those members of the Body of Christ who have me in their hearts. James says there is need for us to confess our faults to one another and then to pray for one another.

Here's the snag. No pain, no gain! If I wish to advance as a disciple, I must submit to strong discipline by other Christians. Who do I know that loves me enough to function that way? They need to know about my self confessed faults so that they can treat me accordingly. They need to take me on as a work in progress and to give me no peace until they see positive development. Who is prepared to do it? Who is prepared to give me that amount of time and prayerful attention?

We are so busy engaged in Church affairs, few of us have time to give for training each other and being trained ourselves. Surely this is to admit defeat. How can athletes even compete if they are ill disciplined and thoroughly unfit? How can an army be successful if the troops are flabby, ill disciplined and lacking in know-how when facing the foe?

The fear of rejection figures in this. Do you want to risk losing my friendship by speaking firmly ... let alone, *acting* firmly ... in order to get me free of the faults I confess to you?

Who said true discipleship was cosy?

A determined team got Matt Baker through. He did well, but so did his team. It was truly a team effort. We saw huge amounts of evidence for team work in the Olympic Games. Can we not draw obvious lessons from it? How can we expect to put to death what is earthly in us without help? The faults or expressions of iniquity in the heart (call them what you will) have no place in the Church that hopes to be victorious. We are responsible for dealing with the problem.

Let's go to it.

Chapter Thirteen

Safety in numbers

The battle front in Spiritual Warfare is much wider than we think. Each one of us is in the front line and the conflict is continuous. So we cannot relax even for a moment. If we do, we're done! This explains our Lord's insistence, everywhere reflected in the Bible, that we are to resist the devil and stand firm against him (*Ephesians 6:13ff* [HISTEMI: stand]; *James 4:7b; 1 Peter 5:9* [ANTHISTEMI: stand against, resist]) while at the same time we are to attack Satan's kingdom forces and strongholds to release his prisoners (*Lk 9:1-2; 10:19; 1 Jn 2:13-14*).

Total war is what we're talking about as reflected in *Matthew 16:18*, where the Greek word translated "overcome" has a double thrust: it means "cannot withstand" as well as "cannot defeat". So if we are an expression of the Church Jesus builds, founded firmly upon *him*, and *only* him, we are given power and authority both to defeat Satan's forces when we attack them and to resist them when they attack us.

The true Church is a warfaring Church: we are born for battle and the conflict can be up close and personal. But we are blessed in being part of the Body of Christ. We are not fighting our battles alone. We are stronger when we stand shoulder to shoulder.

But the devil does not want us standing shoulder to shoulder because he can pick us off more easily when we are isolated from each other. If he can keep us isolated he can control and manipulate us with consummate ease.

Our unity is therefore a critical factor in spiritual warfare.

"Have you heard ...?"
In this chapter and the next I want to deal with the matter of betrayal and loss of confidentiality.

We are all familiar with films and books in which Catholic priests flatly refuse to divulge the 'secrets of the Confessional' even to Police Officers! When it happens priests are severely criticised for obstructing the course of justice. But they always appeal to a higher authority, believing this is God's way for pastoral ministry. It has a ring of truth about it. Maintaining confidences is not always a strong feature amongst Christians: even those calling themselves "disciples". There is something utterly delicious in divulging confidences: usually under pretence that we are doing it for the victim's good!

"I was told this in confidence, but I feel I should share it with *you* because I know you'll pray about it!"

That at least has an *appearance* of virtue, but far too often we release information simply in order to curry favour or, at its most perverse, to cripple a brother or sister's reputation to further our own. It's incredible but the behaviour of some Christians can be downright evil at times.

Betraying confidences is a reflection of the sad condition of many Churches and fellowship groups, of whatever size. It undermines their effectiveness because confession of faults – areas of personal vulnerability – to each other is an essential part of Body life. James makes that clear (*James 5:16*). Fear of being betrayed will stifle any fellowship and makes confession of genuine faults impossible. This produces a group shallow at best and impotent at worst.

One contributory factor regarding gossip and the betrayal of confidences is *remoteness from each other.* In a traditional church congregation there is often a very low level of personal interaction between the members. Many scarcely know each other. It gives the Lord a major problem. At any rate it does if his own words are taken seriously. Here is *John 13:34: "A new commandment I give you: LOVE ONE ANOTHER AS I HAVE LOVED YOU."*

We're good at having meetings, but very bad at meeting. I love the song written by Robin and Julie Hawkins:
"Come, come, come to the meeting:
Give everyone a greeting: I'm sorry it's so fleeting
But I've got another meeting and I'm late already now!"

Seeing Church as family
In today's world we have come to evaluate virtually everything from an individualistic perspective. Self expression, self reliance, self satisfaction, self pity, self confidence … Chambers Dictionary lists at least 100 words with 'self' as a prefix.

The majority of the words are not positive attributes at all and reflect this attitude so beloved by fans of Frank Sinatra: "I did it *my* way!"

One of the first things God ever said about man was, *"It is not good for man to be alone"* (*Genesis 2:18*). It applied in the first instance to Adam's marriage to Eve, but the principle goes much further. The entire Bible is about relationship – God with his people and his people with each other. We are created for relationship with God and with others like ourselves: God's children. But as soon as we come into a relationship of any kind it means we have to make adjustments to our life style, and we don't like doing that. It's well demonstrated in marriage. Moses said *"the two become one flesh"* (*Genesis 2:24*). That's picked up by Paul in *Ephesians 5:31*. It's very profound and absolutely basic: but it implies massive changes in thinking and behaving.

The same principle is there in *Romans 12:5* where Paul wrote *"we being many are one body in Christ, and individually members of one another"*. Again, that implies massive changes in thinking and behaving. We are not isolated believers: we are individually members of one another. Like it or not we are joined in relationship and can only function properly when we submit to that fact and live in the reality of it. In the same way that my marriage would be poverty stricken if I viewed becoming one flesh with Lindy simply as a description of living in the same house, so too being members of one another in the Body of Christ has to mean more than attending meetings together.

Being one flesh with Lindy is secure, intimate and profoundly fulfilling but it means an abandonment of my independence. It is costly and intensely demanding at every level of life – hers and mine.

Being Church is like that. We belong together as members of the Body of Christ. The joys are wonderful but they do not come cheap!

God loves the principle of family. The family is God's principal metaphor for Christians' relationship with him and with each other.

- We become God's children when we're born again (*John 1:12; Romans 8:16;1 John 3:2*)
- We're members of his household (*Ephesians 2:19*)
- Jesus came to reveal God as Father (*Luke 11:2; John 1:18;16:25*)
- Jesus sent the Spirit, among other wonderful things, to reveal God as our intimate Abba (*Romans 8:14; Galatians 4:6*)
- Christians are regularly referred to in the New Testament as brothers (*Matthew 23:8; Acts 6:3; 1 Peter 1:22; 1 John 3:14, 16*)
- One of the most poignant descriptions of Jesus and his Church is the relationship between a bride and groom (*Matthew 9:15; John 3:29; 2 Corinthians 11:2; Ephesians 5:22-33*)

So every expression of "church" needs to express "family". Here are some features of family life that spring to mind:

- Devotion to parents
- Enveloping each other in love
- Contributing to the family purse
- Applauding our siblings' personal achievements
- Encouraging each other when discouraged
- Standing together against outside forces
- Teaching the younger ones
- Learning wisdom under Father's headship
- Enjoying each other and relaxing together
- Speaking kindly to each other
- Speaking kindly of each other
- Speaking firmly to each other when necessary
- Keeping each other up to the mark
- Using our strengths for the good of all
- Not allowing familiarity to breed contempt
- Closing ranks and showing loyalty
- Pulling together in doing chores and messy things
- Fraternal, good natured rivalry

These are among the features of family life. They should also figure in our relationships in the Body of Christ.

Fear of betrayal is a principal hindrance to sharing our lives with other believers. We hesitate to go beyond a certain point because we cannot be sure that what we have shared will not be gossiped abroad. All too often our hesitation has a solid base to it – previous experience has taught us to be cautious … and taught us well!

Gossip is one of the principal brakes on our spiritual growth as churches and fellowship groups. It has to be addressed.

The true story is told of an African preacher whose ministry was ruined by gossip. Churches in which he had previously proclaimed the Word were suddenly barred to him. It transpired that a man he had challenged over marriage unfaithfulness was determined to get back at him and so he spread it about that the preacher had himself been sexually perverse. Hence the closed doors.

The preacher challenged the gossiper who had so damaged his reputation and integrity. At first the man denied it, but then, under pressure and conviction, admitted his guilt.

The preacher suggested they go for a walk together. On the way he purchased a chicken and much to the gossiper's surprise asked him to pluck it as they walked. This he did and the feathers scattered to the four winds. As they reached the end of the walk and the chicken carcase was plucked bare, the preacher turned for home. As he and the gossiper walked home the preacher said, "My brother, will you please stick back the feathers you scattered?"

Food for thought!

Chapter Fourteen

Radical faith please!

When Lord Norman Tebbit was a Member of the House of Commons he distinguished himself as a penetrating thinker and able Government Minister. I recently heard him being interviewed on the radio. He said that standing up and speaking in the House was a daunting business because he had the Opposition Members facing him *and quite a number of enemies on the benches behind him!*

It's a bit like the Church. It's one thing to have opposition from the devil and his cohorts, but quite another when we are assailed by other Christians. The activity of some of our own back-benchers (and front benchers as well) can sometimes be very hurtful and devastating in its impact on biblical truth and practice.

I saw a remarkable film the other day. Though entitled *The Daniel Project*, it is not an overtly Christian film, but it aims to put biblical prophecy under a journalistic microscope. Remarkable conclusions are drawn from this penetrating critique that leads the main presenter, a self confessed sceptic, to reconsider his position. However, in one comment he made, the presenter expressed shock when he learned that many so-called Christians and Christian leaders do not accept the teaching of the Bible. He assumed that *all* Christians read and believe the Bible! Not any more!

The Falling away

Paul spoke about a rebellion (Greek: APOSTASIS) that will happen before the coming of the Lord and our being gathered to him (*1 Thessalonians 4:16*-17 and 2 *Thessalonians 2:1-3*). The word APOSTASIS actually means 'falling away' from something. So the rebellion spoken of is a falling away. What from? Taken in context it can only be God's Word – the Truth.

Is it happening? Tragically, yes. And not only amongst Churchmen of the more liberal way of thinking: there is a tendency even among some Evangelicals to sit loose upon certain biblical truths that are considered extreme or inconvenient.

There is a war on. Some are suggesting that insistence upon correct doctrine is a comparatively modern phenomenon in the Church and that authentic Christianity has to do with feeding the hungry and meeting the needs of the poor. Well it *does,* but not at the expense of Truth! Right believing must be matched by right living. The two are not mutually exclusive. Right living flows from right believing.

Calling in the Doctor

I recall a rare BBC television interview with Dr Martyn Lloyd-Jones. The interviewer asked the great Bible expositor why he never preached sermons on political and social issues. Why his insistence upon Bible exposition and the need for correct doctrine? The Doctor's answer was succinct and very much to the point. He said he preached Bible truth to change a man's heart, and a repentant heart is the only thing that will change a man's life-style. I'll go with that!

Jesus the Radical
Biblical Christianity is radical: it goes right to the roots of our faith. It is, in that sense, intolerant of anything that is not grounded in the Word. We are obliged to speak only the truth: but when we do that it must be bathed in love (*Ephesians 4:15*). The old adage, "Truth hurts" certainly applies to biblical truth when those confronted by it are not prepared to submit their traditions, reason and will to Jesus. The classic example in the ministry of Jesus is *John 6:51-70*. Our Lord had been teaching in the Capernaum synagogue and spoke of himself as *"the living bread that came down from heaven"*. The Jews were outraged. As he expanded on the theme even the disciples started squirming (*60*) and within a short space of time many of his disciples - though not the Twelve - turned back and no longer followed him (*66*).

To live according to the truth requires a radical rethink of our personal relationships within the corporate body of Christ. It requires an honesty sometimes missing from fellowship groups. But when present such honesty enables us to speak only what is true and to speak that truth in love.

Goodbye gossip
One of our most pernicious and destructive tendencies is to delight in gossip. We speak about one another in a manner that understates the truth, embroiders it or exaggerates it.

Misuse of the tongue can be a fire wreaking destruction and death (*James 3:6*).

What does the Bible have to say about gossip? Take, for example, the *Book of Proverbs*.

A gossip betrays a confidence, but a trustworthy man keeps a secret. So says *Proverbs 11:13*. A confidence is a secret shared in order to receive encouragement, comfort, correction and upbuilding. Someone who is faithful to hear and keep the secret is called 'trustworthy', a wonderful quality in a person.

Proverbs 20:19 adds a warning: "*... so avoid a man who talks too much*". We should avoid gossips, even when we are not the victims of their perverse behaviour. The tendency with gossips is that their behaviour is contagious. If we associate with people like that, we can be infected and become gossipy and untrustworthy ourselves. Sometimes the active avoidance of such people is a divine requirement.

A gossip separates close friends
This is *Proverbs 16:28*. How often we see this happen in a church. Sometimes envy of a relationship can lead us to drop a few choice comments at the right time and they serve to break a friendship, thus enabling us to take advantage and move in. The devastation caused can be ruinous because it divides the body of Christ.

A gossip's words are like choice morsels; they go down to a man's inmost parts

Proverbs 18:8 conveys the deliciousness of tittle-tattle. There are those who feed on gossip and find it utterly satisfying and are ravenous for their next meal! When the writer of *Proverbs* speaks of a gossip's words going down into a man's inmost parts, it suggests that he digests those words and they become part of him. The lie, half truth or innuendo lives with him and occupies his thoughts throughout the day and the night. He becomes convinced of the report and it affects him in both his relationship with the victim and the accuser. All those relationships are devastated.

Without wood a fire goes out, without gossip a quarrel dies down
Proverbs 26:20 shows that as logs tossed into a fire keep it blazing so too a quarrel is inflamed by uninformed and mischievous comment.

Solomon was penetrating in his writing of the book of *Proverbs*. His was the voice of experience. After all, Solomon had a thousand women in his life and we can only begin to imagine the level of gossip that went on in his harem as girls sought to outdo one another! When it came to gossip, I reckon King Solly knew a thing or two about its effects!

References in the New Testament
There are several Greek words translated as "gossip". Shades of meaning fill out our understanding and enable us to resist the temptation with every fibre of our being. It requires that level of diligence because the impact of gossip can destroy a church. In consequence the devil is very keen on it.

Romans 1:29 *"... they have become filled with every kind of wickedness ... they are gossips, slanderers, God-haters, insolent, arrogant and boastful ..."*

Paul is writing about the godless and wicked in the world who God has given over to depravity. He describes their disgusting excesses and in amongst them is 'gossips'. The Greek is PSITHURIST<u>E</u>S, a word to describe a whisperer or tale bearer. The first syllable lends the word a sibilant quality not unlike the hissing of a snake! Perhaps this helps to identify whispering and tale-bearing as a definite ploy of the Serpent. People who engage in gossip are playing into Satan's welcoming arms.

2 Corinthians 12:20
Here Paul uses the same Greek word to identify gossip as a problem, not in this instance amongst the ungodly but incredibly amongst Spirit filled believers in Corinth. That's disappointing isn't it?

Along with gossip he mentions quarrelling, jealousy, outbursts of anger, factions, slander (literally: 'bad speaking'), arrogance and disorder. And this in a church that according to *1 Corinthians 1:7* did not lack any spiritual gift.

I once met a man named Philip Saywell. I thought it a magnificent name for a believer! The word selected by Paul in *2 Corinthians 12:20* and translated as 'slander' is KATALALIA – the precise opposite of 'Say well'.

Saying things that are not good, not godly, is guaranteed to weaken and disqualify us from the ranks of overcomers, rendering us incapable of waging war successfully.

1 Timothy 5:13
Here Paul is addressing certain Christian women of his acquaintance. They are going from house to house gossiping and acting as busybodies. The verb for 'gossiping' in this case is PHLUAREO: and means 'talking nonsense' about someone and bringing 'unsubstantiated charges'.

3 John 10 uses the same word of a renegade Christian named Diotrephes. This man had been spreading malicious gossip about John and his friends. John writes, *"If I come I will call attention to what he is doing."* That is where many of us would chicken out! Sometimes in order to root out this problem of gossip, leaders may have to expose the sin publicly as a warning to the church. Many Christians would run a mile if standards like that were introduced! But this is none other than normal New Testament Church life. Have we pretentions to be a biblical church? If so, this is the sort of issue that we need to confront and deal with.

Food for thought!

Chapter Fifteen

Sleep-walking into deception?

Amongst Jewish people of the First Century there was a very well organised system of Social Security that channelled the alms of the people to the needy through anonymous Temple and synagogue hand-outs. Deserving widows and destitute folks could always count on a weekly allowance: the sense of corporate care within the Jewish community was very strong.

But something dramatic had happened to the Jewish community. It had been split apart by a significant rift. A number of Jewish people had embraced 'The Way'. Viewed as a messianic cult originating in Jerusalem this movement was storming through Israel at an alarming rate.

Mind you, these followers of Jesus the Nazarene were paying a heavy price for their faith. Amongst other things they automatically disqualified themselves from receiving support from Jewish social funding. Naturally, the destitute and widows without families were hardest hit. They had nothing and now could expect nothing. It was very serious. If the situation were not addressed, it would result in deteriorating health, starvation and even death. The price of serving Jesus as Lord and Messiah was heavy.

To address the emergency, the young church in Jerusalem had started a food bank to provide for widows in the fellowship, but nepotism arose and drastic measures were required to correct things by appointing deacons in the fledgling church (*Acts 6:1-6*). The removal of Jewish social benefits lies behind the apostles' insistent demand that providing for widows and the disadvantaged must be a prominent feature of Word-led and Spirit-led churches (*1Timothy 5:4-9; James 1:27*).

It is this kind of nitty-gritty reality that provokes me and shows me that true faith in Jesus Christ has always carried enormous consequences, not least at the social level.

Is that something that will come into British society at some stage soon? The removal of our right to Social Security benefits could well be a mere step away because of our perceived "anti-social" beliefs regarding other religions, evolution, abortion, euthanasia and homosexual behaviour (for instance). Once public opinion is inflamed, the politicians could move against us very quickly.

Bye-bye, 'Bye-byes'!
Speaking of these things forces me to conclude that it is later than we think. Many sermons, recordings, books and television preachers warn us about the realities of the end times, and while we recognise the truth and applaud the call to arms, we have a strange resistance to acknowledging that THE BATTLE IS NOW!

Many of us have an unfortunate air of detachment – almost a paralysis. We recognise the signs of the times but we are strangely mesmerised: lulled into a dream-like state where we want so badly to fight but we are held down as if by chains. It is as if a sleeping sickness holds us in thrall ... then, out of the darkness and into our dreams, 'Bugler Paul' blasts Reveille!

"The hour has come for you to wake up from your slumber, because our salvation is nearer now than when we first believed. The night is nearly over; the day is almost here. So let us put aside the deeds of darkness and put on the armour of light. Let us behave decently, as in the daytime; not in orgies and drunkenness, not in sexual immorality and debauchery, not in dissension and jealousy. Rather clothe yourselves with the Lord Jesus Christ, and do not think about how to gratify the desires of the sinful nature" (Romans 14:11-14).

I REALLY WISH HE WOULDN'T DO THAT! It is so disturbing! I'm not sure I *want* to be woken up because when I wake up, I'm straight back into the state of consciousness and reality I left. Back into the thick of the battle.

At other levels of life, we will go frantic in our attempts to revive a person who has lost consciousness. But for some perverse reason, when it comes to spiritual matters, we rest content in each other's indolence. The reason may be that we are all snoozing around the tent pole together, not wishing to disturb our fellow warriors and certainly not wishing to be disturbed ourselves! Bliss!

The snag is that while we slumber the enemy is swarming all over the camp! Discipleship is tough.

Even after fifty years of discipleship, I never realised until recently just how tough it can be to live by faith. When I say, "live by faith" I am not referring to money: I am speaking about the day to day slog of keeping awake and doing what Paul said in *Romans 13* (quoted above). To keep doggedly moving forward takes iron determination and a certainty that "The Lord is here: his Spirit is with us".

A few generations ago, disciples of Jesus spoke of periods of severe testing as being "the dark night of the soul": the devil accusing them of being a failure on many fronts. He loves to discourage us and to keep us cowed.

Some of Satan's accusations are lies and I can resist those quite easily by confessing the appropriate part of God's written Word and standing on it. But certain other accusations may well be justified, so it is futile for me to deny those. As regards those matters I must repent, put things right as best I can and then rest in the propitiating sacrifice of my Saviour. Then I can move on in His victory, confessing the truth of God's reassuring promises as I go. Hallelujah! But let nobody say it's easy! It is warfare, after all.

How serious am I about being a successful warrior? Is the rallying call, "Back to the Word!" a summons I drive myself to obey?

In the heat of battle, confusion is all around. Fighting our way out of the confusion is never straightforward. Perhaps this is what Jesus meant when he said repeatedly that deception would be a sign of the last days (*Matt 24:4, 5, 11*, etc.).

Deception and confusion are close relatives. When we are in a confused state we are easily deceived. Confusion is a lack of clarity in thinking. It is produced when we move away from the certainties of the Word and it is encouraged by Satan, the arch-strategist. Where Satan dominates, confusion is always present.

God's warrior is difficult to live with because he is not prepared to lie down alongside snoozers or even tolerate them! Before long his continual provocation makes them feel exceedingly uncomfortable and they either wake up themselves or withdraw into that beckoning, cosy sleeping bag – their comfort zone – and get their heads down again.

God's warrior is always bellicose as he seeks to encourage his fellows, and they often don't like that. Warfare is continually on his mind and this disturbs the indolent. All they want is the talk and not the power. But for that to change, a sense of urgency has to be recovered, coupled with the determination to get real with God.

The devil never lets up
A drunken motorist was stopped by a policeman. "Didn't you see the arrows?" The drunk replied, "Arrows, Offisher? I didn't even see the Indians!"

Much as we experience the pains of attack, many are reluctant to acknowledge that Satan has an involvement in so much of it. If truth be told, many of us prefer not to even think about the devil. However, the fact remains that the devil is prowling around all the time, seeking someone to devour. That's Peter's assessment recorded in *1 Peter 5:8-9*:

"Be self-controlled and alert. Your enemy the devil prowls around like a roaring lion looking for someone to devour. Resist him, standing firm in your faith, because you know that your brothers throughout the world are undergoing the same kind of sufferings."

Many of us have long since given up functioning as warriors who live with the certainty that they are surrounded by satanic forces. We imagine that we have moved beyond such archaic thinking. In fact we rather pity those poor souls who still reckon on the need to minister deliverance and to be protecting themselves from the devil and all his works. We recoil in embarrassment to think of those we used to describe as "seeing demons under every bed"! Remember *them*? My word, I'm glad *they* left the church!

Many Evangelicals and their leaders today act and speak as though the devil is "yesterday's news". Well, he is NOT! The devil is alive and well and hell-bent on wounding, silencing and defeating us. This is his constant activity. He never lets up in his offensive.

It was the well loved David Watson who wrote, "The scholars have voted the devil out

And so, of course, he's gone!
But simple folks would like to know
'Who carries his business on?'"

However much we protest that all talk of Satan and demons is primitive, disturbing and downright irrelevant, we cannot escape one obvious fact – *the devil is wreaking carnage and the evidence is everywhere, both in society and in the churches.*

We can try to argue him out of the picture, we can divert ourselves with all manner of exciting church activities, we can invest our time in mission programmes, learn new songs, read new books, watch new 'Christian' celebrities on the tele … keep ourselves busy with church activities every night of the week, and fail to see the awful yet obvious truth – *the devil is still hard at work and fighting for dear life – YOUR dear life and mine!*

Spiritual warfare is not his occasional activity, it is his constant activity and should be ours too. If it was so for the Lord it is so for us. But Satan is at his most dangerous when we act as if he and his demons have given up and retired from the field.

We need to wake up, throw back our bedclothes, get dressed in our armour and engage the enemy. That lethargy you experience as you try to pray and study the Word is warfare. You need to fight it in the Name of Jesus. That desire to be private and not to confess your faults to others is warfare. You need to fight it in the Name of Jesus.

That reluctance to speak truth when in the presence of lies and blasphemy is warfare. You need to speak in the Name of Jesus.

Pressing through when every fibre of my being is screaming for repose is the stuff of overcoming faith.

It's later than we think.

Chapter Sixteen

Fit for Purpose

Olympic mania

Now consigned to the pages of history, the XXXth Olympiad of the modern era of the Olympic Games provided us with great memories of athletic prowess. Records tumbled, medals were awarded, fame shed its spotlight on the few. We were all impressed by the astonishing achievements of fit young folk prepared to be trained and disciplined to such an exalted level.

In the ancient world, sporting events were linked to survival. The ability to shoot, run, fight or throw was all geared to life and death. In the lives of Bible characters like David and Jonathan skill with slings and arrows was honed through hours of devoted practice. Their aim was victory over enemies and predators.

The emergence of the Greeks as a world power brought a fresh look to sporting ability. No longer was its purpose seen simply as a necessary activity to keep one sharp and able to provide for and defend oneself and one's family, but now it became less utilitarian and developed into a form of entertainment. More than that, athletic prowess displayed the beauty of the human form and this appealed to the Greek mindset.

The Olympic Games started around 776 BC and were held in the Valley of Elis in the shadow of Mount Olympus in south west Greece. There was a religious element: the thousands who gathered honoured Zeus, the king of the gods.

All this athletic activity meant that the level of achievement was astonishing and city states vied with each other to produce the best performers in field and track, rewarding them with honours and treating them like pop-stars! Athens and Corinth hosted the major Games and competitiveness between the cities sometimes led to real animosity!

When the Romans conquered Greece in 146BC, Greek culture exerted a profound influence on Roman life and once the years of the Republic were at an end and Augustus became Emperor in 27BC, Imperial Rome embraced Hellenistic ideas with abandon. The Emperors encouraged athletics and the arts and in every corner of the Empire sports arenas of various types were constructed. The Olympics, founded in 776BC, continued to flourish in Athens for over 1100 years and it was not until 393AD that Christian Emperor Theodosius abolished them as a pagan aberration.

The Olympics were forgotten for 1500 years and were not revived until the end of the 19th Century, when the First Olympiad of the modern era took place in Athens on Sunday, March 24th 1896.

Making the connection
The Olympic Games provided Christians with a remarkable object lesson to encourage active faith. Participating athletes

had disciplined themselves to a level of fitness that enabled them to achieve heights of performance that seem incredible. They trained hard and had trainers that were determined to see them succeed. The results seen on the track and in the field were impressive!

I am certain that when we watched the London Olympics and watch again through TV re-runs those fit young people achieving such great things, most of us have pangs of conscience that we are abusing our own bodies through bad diet and lethargic life style. Oh to be fit! Oh to be in peak condition! Oh to function at the optimum level!

For most of us it will remain a dream and we have to content ourselves with living that dream through the endeavour of others. As runners thundered round the track, I easily imagined myself running too: a longing expressed vicariously in my vivid imagination ... but it was all a fantasy! There was I sitting on the edge of my chair while *they* were out there *doing* it.

I couldn't help but observe, "See how *young* they are!" However hard I tried I could never achieve what they do because my ageing body is beyond that level of training. I've left it far too late ... *years* too late.

Now here's the good news! Ageism is not a factor in the Kingdom of our Lord and Saviour Jesus Christ!

My spiritual athleticism is not limited by my physical limitations. And here, surely, is the most wonderful challenge.

All those young Olympic athletes had a shared aim: to win. Although the achievement of gaining a Silver or Bronze medal is extraordinary, all will have striven to achieve the Gold! For them, the Gold standard is the *only* standard! To aim for less than the Gold guarantees you will never win it.

The ultimate aim

For those of us who have pretensions to be overcomers for Christ – true disciples – we have to have a settled aim. What *is* our aim? To be part of a truly successful church? A church that is alive rather than dead; awake rather than asleep; in truth rather than in error?

The quest to find expressions of Church as it is meant to be takes us into some fascinating corners of history. Where do we look to find the authentic expressions of Church?

Some would take us back to the very early days of the Charismatic Movement, when things were really popping and believers were devoted to God's Word as much as to his Spirit. Others would push us further back to the days of the Wesley brothers, George Whitefield and the heady days of the 18th Century Awakening. Others again would urge us to return to the great upheavals of the 16th Century Reformation.

"Those were the days! Oh, that we were *there*!" Or, "Oh, that they were *here*!"

A more recent tide of opinion is pushing us back to the New Testament churches. This appears to be preferable because the biblical Church must surely be the correct model. First Century churches must provide the blueprint for us to follow.

But it ain't necessarily so! Even a casual glance through the New Testament at Letters addressed to churches will show that all was not well with them. With the single exception of *Philippians*, where the greatest problem appears to have been a 'tiff' between two of the women (*Philippians 4:2*), the rest were beset with challenging problems: some of them extremely serious. *(Romans 2:1-11; 1 Corinthians 1:10-12; 3:1-4; 5:1-2; Galatians 1:6-7; Colossians 2:20-23; 2 Thessalonians 3:11-15; Revelation 2:1-3:22)*

While we are obviously meant to learn from these examples of Church, we must be careful to discern what is good from what is bad. So merely to cry, "Back to biblical Church!" may not be as appropriate or wise as we might think.

So what do we do? Clearly we have to do something! Things are very far from right in our churches and in our personal walk of faith, so where do we look for help?

The answer is so obvious that I will be accused of being simplistic. But after years of experience and frustration I conclude that the answer has to be JESUS! Now *there's* a surprise!

In describing our Christian faith-life, the writer of *Hebrews* likens it to running in a great athletics event.

I refer, of course, to *Hebrews 12:1-13*, where readers are provoked to persevere and submit to discipline. Success is not easily achieved and discipline must be welcomed as a friend. The crowning revelation comes in *12:2*: *"Let us fix our eyes on Jesus, the pioneer and perfecter of our faith"*.

The strength of the word "fix" is such that we understand that looking at Jesus is to be our constant aim. I am led to think of an eagle spotting its prey. From the moment it sees it, the eagle's eyes are focused and fixed on nothing else. The great bird swoops down, and as it streaks through the air it sees nothing but the prey. That way lies success in the hunt.

The *Hebrews* revelation concerning the Games is timely is it not? As we watched the athletes performing, the images created powerful illustrations of the biblical text. Had we been able to watch a race from behind the finishing tape as the runners came pounding towards us, we would have observed that their eyes were bulging from the sheer effort to keep focused!

Is our focus on Jesus? Is our faith fixed on him? The disciple who is determined to run the race of faith is locked on to Jesus: his eyes never shift.

Many self-confessed believers do not live with Jesus in the centre. They rarely *speak* of him by Name: they rarely *think* of him. They may engage in all manner of "Christian" activity, but what about HIM?
WHAT PLACE HAS JESUS IN YOUR LIFE? Come along, let's get real. One of the (fairly) contemporary songs that we

sing declares, "Jesus, be the centre". It's a good declaration and it's utterly biblical. But do the words sung have any reality in life for us? If I ask Jesus to be the centre, there will be far reaching consequences. Not all of them intended or welcome!

Hebrews 12:2 describes Jesus as the author (pioneer) and perfecter of my faith. In other words, faith starts in Jesus and it will end in Jesus. It is rather like observing the bottom and top rungs of a ladder. But, here's the thing: all the rungs in between are Jesus too! My entire faith race must be motivated by Jesus, saturated in Jesus, enabled by Jesus from start to finish.

Have you noticed that many Christians speak and pray in public without a single reference to Jesus? They mention God, they mention the Lord, they mention Church ... but it often seems that using the name of Jesus sticks in the throat and is an embarrassment. Perhaps the time has come for us to change that. In the 1960s a group of young believers emerged from the Hippy scene. They called themselves "Jesus People". Remember them? They were lively and had a non-conformity about them that many of us more traditional believers found fascinating. Many of them were soundly converted to Jesus, though, sadly, some later went astray from the Scriptures in their quest for freedom. But I loved the title! "Jesus People"!

Fixing my eyes on Jesus may well mean
1)   Using his dear Name far more in my prayers;

2) Using his dear Name far more in my conversations with fellow believers;
3) Using his dear Name with my family and work colleagues;
4) Using his dear Name when speaking with non-believers.

Do you find some of those suggestions appealing or appalling!

Food for thought!

Chapter Seventeen

A true and painful story

I've known him for years. He's a Dutchman. But his name – Jacob – shows he is a Jew. Jacob lived with his family in Israel and was engaged in the tourism industry until commercial pressures resulting from the Intifada forced them back to the family home in Amsterdam.

Jacob has little time for Christians or the Church. Given his experiences you can't wonder at it. When working as an Israeli Licensed Guide Jacob guided many Christian groups from a variety of countries, mainly America. With certain fine exceptions, what he saw did not impress him. He met many tour leaders, pastors, preachers and televangelists: often spending time with them "off duty". When relaxed they sometimes showed Jacob a side to their personality that failed to impress him.

Being a professional Israeli Guide Jacob knows a great deal about Jesus. What he knows he greatly admires. He readily admits that had he been alive in Jesus' day he would almost certainly have become a committed disciple, never mind the cost.

So why is Jacob not a Jewish Christian? Or, as we fashionably say, a Messianic Believer? Theologically Jacob cannot accept that Jesus is alive and at the moment he is still stuck in that doubt. But there are other barriers that include certain experiences with Christians.

On one occasion when leading a large American group whose minister had a large American ministry, he was taken aside by the minister who said he would like to baptise Jacob in the Jordan. Jacob protested that this was preposterous because he is a Jew and not a Christian. Whereupon the minister 'came clean' and admitted that he wanted it to happen because the people would love it and it would mean that the group members could return home and say they had "baptised the Guide". It would provide a wonderful boost for further groups to sign up to his Israel tours.

Jacob could not hide his disgust. So as a final persuader the minister offered Jacob $1,000 to 'go along' with the stunt.

Jacob was so shocked and upset he turned on his heel and walked away in tears. He never went back to the group. The minister was left standing there in the middle of the Coach parking lot with his mouth open! I would like to think something unpleasant came along and filled it for him!

Jacob (not his real name) is still seeking Jesus. Pray for him.

The battle for integrity
They tell me that 'discipleship' is an in-topic amongst churches at the moment. That's good, so long as the word is not being debased in order to accommodate it in church programmes! Our Lord did not tell us to be religious, he told

us to be disciples and to make disciples (Matthew 28:19). By definition a *math*e̲*t*e̲*s* (Greek) is a follower and learner. A disciple of Jesus follows His every move and obeys His every word. That's commitment and it is foundational of genuine discipleship. The New Testament knows no half measures.

This is what drove the Wesley brothers, George Whitefield and others to form the 'Holy Club' at Oxford in the 18th Century. Although a derogatory term coined by their enemies it fairly describes their motivation. They strove to be holy: separated out for the glory of Jesus. In order to become this they applied rigorously the injunction of Jesus expressed in the little letter written by his half-brother (*James 5:16*), *"Confess your faults to each other and pray for each other so that you may be healed …."*

Set in the context of prayer for the sick it is, none the less, a principle of wider application that cements and enlarges the deep relationship that needs to exist between disciples of Christ. We are called to a life of truth in which there can be no hypocrisy at any level. Integrity and discipleship go hand in hand.

Confession of "faults" is not confession of "sins". Sins are the outward expression of faults. James does not tell us to air our dirty linen in public by giving vivid details of our sins.

All that does is to provide people with delicious mind pictures and ammunition to be held for future use against us! Our faults, on the other hand, are areas of weakness that drive us to commit actual sins. Our sins are the consequence of giving in to these inner 'drivers'.

In the natural world a fault is a weakness in the earth's crust that gives rise to earthquakes. Scaled up to the human level, our faults erupt in sins. This is picked up by Jesus in the Sermon on the Mount. According to Matthew 5:21-22 and 27-28, it is anger that provides the driver for murder and lust that provides the driver for adultery. That is not rocket science: it is plain teaching and simple to understand.

If I have the mastery over my anger there is no possibility of my committing murder. If I put lust to death, Lindy need never fear that I shall be unfaithful to her.

Along with anger and lust, the faults that left untreated can have devastating consequences include selfish ambition, pride, envy, criticism, resentment, bitterness, hatred, greediness for money and possessions, party spirit and so forth. These are areas of weakness that we need to acknowledge, face up to and confess to trusted fellow disciples. It is only when others are aware of our faults that they can stand with us, providing encouragement through prayer and strong exhortation that is thoroughly Bible-based.

In Colossians 3:5, Paul says, *"Put to death, therefore, whatever belongs to your earthly nature"*.

He then illustrates what he means: *"fornication, impurity, lust, evil desires and greed, which is idolatry."*

So this "earthly nature" is revealed through our faults. And Paul insists *these faults must be put to death*!

This sounds well and good – and obviously *is* – but how is it done? For instance, how do I put lust to death?

I was pondering over this and pondering shifted into praying (!). Quite suddenly I felt the Lord slip something into my mind that was not there before. I felt he was telling me to treat lust as though it were a weed in the garden! Putting weeds to death can be done in two ways: by depriving them of light and water and also by treating them with poison. It may sound curious to you, but I found the thought an enormous help.

Smother weeds
Deny them water and sunlight and weeds cannot survive. In terms of dealing with lust it means I have to deprive it of anything that might feed and stimulate it. That is not easily done in an age when we are bombarded with sexual images and perverse attitudes. It is all too easy to be caught unawares through watching a TV programme or trailing through the papers or Internet. Lust is stimulated and sin easily comes out. So in practical terms I have to guard what I see and hear as much as possible. I know myself too well to pretend that I can allow overt sexual stimulants to have access.

We were in Amsterdam recently and it was suggested that I be taken to the so-called Red Light District. It sounded like a worthy idea: to be made aware of the sad life lived by prostitutes and to see them advertising their bodies in shop windows. The idea was that it would stimulate prayer.

It might be in order for some believers to go to view such a sight, but I know that for *me* it would have been extremely unwise, not to say dangerous to my spirit. That is because I am aware of lust as an area of personal vulnerability that must not be stimulated. I have to put it to death and depriving it of unrighteous stimulants is crucial.

Poison weeds:
You have to be careful with poisons in the garden. Selective weed killers are the best because they target specific species of plant.

Are you getting the message? The Scriptures are the general means by which *"what belongs to my earthly nature"* can be killed off. And the particular Word to which the Lord leads me is the *selective* means by which it can be done.

It is a wonderful experience when the Holy Spirit shines His revelation through a verse or passage of Scripture and makes it intensely personal. The Word of God becomes like a razor sharp stiletto, slipping through me and penetrating the exact area of my earthly nature that needs dealing with. In just the same way that Jesus got the victory during his temptation in the Wilderness, it is when I am made aware of particular, relevant Scripture passages that I am able to confess them aloud, being confident that God's *rhema* Word*** will see Satan defeated (compare *Luke 4:1-14*).

Our Lord Jesus *lived* in the truth he was confessing: that is the secret for me too. The mere recitation of familiar and relevant

Scriptures will not achieve my purpose. It is the life lived in the *application* of the Word that sees death to iniquity and sin.

Here, of course, we see the added contribution to be made by our brothers and sisters: those engaged alongside us in the pursuit of true holiness. When I confess my faults it creates the environment for the Holy Spirit to inspire particular and relevant Scriptures to be shared and ministered to me: praying them in vigorously. Admittedly this is a far cry from the sort of activity we are more accustomed to in our prayer meetings and home fellowship meetings, but discipleship of the Jesus variety requires a fresh approach.

Robust discipleship of the non-religious variety is what attracted my friend Jacob to Jesus. I'm not really surprised. It is just a crying shame there appears to be so little of it around today!

How about it?

*** The New Testament uses two terms for God's "Word": *logos* (as in *Hebrews 4:12*) and *rhema* (as in *Ephesians 6:17*).
Logos should be seen as the complete revelation of God's Word (the entire Bible) while *rhema* describes particular parts of the Bible conveyed to us by the Holy Spirit at particular times for particular purposes.

Chapter Eighteen

Dealing with my fear

The Saint's call to arms is found in *Ephesians 6:10-18*. Depending upon our spiritual readiness it can inspire us with faith or fill us with fear! Fear of being hurt is the result of an inadequate view of God.

Fear immobilises us. That is why the Bible is filled with the injunction, "Be not afraid!"

When *we* tell one another, "Don't be afraid!" it is often based on nothing except wishful thinking. When *God* says it, it's another matter entirely! There is a solid reason behind it. It is not simply a stark command with nothing to support it. Our faith stands on the solid ground of God's promises. We do not fear BECAUSE …

Consider the weight of God's support under these divine statements. Fear is banished in the presence of such assurances!

*Genesis 15:1 "Do not be afraid, Abram, **I am your shield, your very great reward.**"*
Genesis 21:17 "What is the matter, Hagar? Do not be afraid; God has heard the boy crying as he lies there. Lift the boy up

*and take him by the hand, **for I will make him into a great nation.*** *"*

Genesis 26:24 t *"... the Lord appeared to Isaac and said, "I am The God of your father Abraham.* ***Do no be afraid, for I am with you; I will bless you and will increase the number of your descendants for the sake of my servant Abraham."***

*Genesis 46:3-4 "God spoke to Jacob and said, "Do not be afraid to go down to Egypt, **for I will make you into a great nation there. I will go down to Egypt with you, and I will surely bring you back again.***"*

*Joshua 1:9 "Have I not commanded you? Be strong and courageous. Do not be terrified; do not be discouraged. **For the Lord your God will be with you wherever you go.***"*

Our Lord Jesus frequently commanded his disciples, *"Do not be afraid!"* But there was an undergirding reason: Jesus was *with* them. His presence gave them courage and assurance in the face of opposition. See, for instance, *Matthew 10:29-31; 14:22-33; 17:7; 28:10* and *Mark 4:35-5:1 (cf 6:50).*

Acts 18:9-11 provides a further example. Here Paul is addressed in a vision from heaven: *"Do not be afraid: keep on speaking, do not be silent. For I am with you ..."*

Then there is *Revelation 1:17 "Do not be afraid! I am the First and the Last. I am He that lives; I was dead, and behold I am alive for ever and ever! And I hold the Keys of death and Hades.*

It doesn't get better than that! DO NOT BE AFRAID!

True courage results from seeing God as he really is.
Paul states, *"Be strong in the Lord and in the power of His might"* (*Ephesians 6:10*). The outcome of the battle rests not on *my* skill or strength, but on *God's* performance!

Our great task is to *"be strong"*, but strong *in the strength of the Lord.* (See *Joshua 1:6, 7, 9; 2 Chronicles 32:7; Isaiah 35:4*).

An earthly general depends upon the strength of his army. The Lord's army is dependant on HIS strength! Without us, the Lord can accomplish his greatest purposes very easily: without HIM we can accomplish nothing at all! That sobering, humbling truth is borne out in passages like *Psalm 144:1-2*.

Our Lord put the matter starkly in *John 15:5*: *"Without me you can do nothing!"* Paul confessed this sobering truth when writing to the Corinthians (*2 Corinthians 3:5*): *"Not that we are competent in ourselves to claim anything for ourselves, but our competence comes from God."* Then again he says to the Philippians (*2:13*), *"Work out your salvation with fear and trembling, for it is God who works in you to will and to act according to his good purpose."*

We need the Lord's strength all the time. If He were to let go of us, we would instantly fall. Even our understanding of the Scriptures is dependent upon God's strength: and, according to *Romans 8:26*, so is prayer.

Inspiration in the jail

John Bunyan was inspired to write "Pilgrim's Progress" in Bedford jail. Paul's great faith builder was written in a jail in Rome. It is commonly supposed that the inspiration for Paul's great teaching on the whole armour of God came from the presence of Roman military guards in his cell. There is a better model!

In *Ephesians 6* Paul states the obvious: *"Finally be strong in the Lord and in HIS mighty power. Put on the full armour OF GOD"*. Paul's primary inspiration is not a Roman sentry! It is the Lord himself! Paul's whole life was saturated with the written Word of God – the Hebrew Scriptures. From infancy he had memorised huge amounts. The Books of the Law, the Prophets and the Writings were his constant food and inspiration: so it is hardly likely that this divine resource would be usurped by a Roman sentry slouched against the cell wall!

Paul's inspiration came from the Word. To a highly trained Jewish theologian like Paul, the prophecies of Isaiah would have been his daily companions. Consider *Isaiah 59:17*: *"(The Lord) put on righteousness as his breastplate, and the helmet of salvation on his head; he put on the garments of vengeance and wrapped himself in zeal as in a cloak."*

Consider also *Isaiah 11:4-5*, a remarkable messianic passage that refers to the Lord Jesus: *"He will strike the earth with the rod of his mouth; with the breath of his mouth he will slay the wicked. Righteousness will be his belt and faithfulness the sash round his waist."*

Spiritual armour is the armour that the Lord has and that he uses to defeat Satan and his forces. It is effective! He makes it available to us and as soon as we enter the lists, the Lord uses his glorious weaponry to wreak havoc and defeat on the enemy through us!

Paul's inspiration in that Roman jail was not some morose legionary or centurion, it was the living Lord whom he served and who filled him with his Spirit! I dare say his faith burst out in a great paeon of praise, *"May GOD arise and may his enemies be scattered!" (Psalm 68:1)*

The final word
Ephesians 6:10 begins with the word *"finally"*. It's a word we preachers use towards the end of a sermon in order to drag people's attention back to the matter in hand! The congregation awakes from slumber with the thought that the end is nigh!

Columbo, the television sleuth, often takes that approach at the end of an interview with a suspect. As he's about to leave the person's office or home, he'll say "O excuse me, Sir, there's just one other thing …" It catches the person off guard and it usually turns out to be pivotal to the case!

In the previous sections of Ephesians Paul has been writing about basic and practical matters: our secure relationship with Jesus, church unity, living as children of God in marriage, parenting and work. It's all demanding stuff, but it's everyday stuff … then comes the *coup de gras*! *"Finally!"*

All these everyday things are in truth a battlefield between us and the devil. The readers would not have seen that coming! Clearly the devil is out to destroy all these familiar things: our faith, our marriage, our family, our testimony ... everything needs to be seen as prospective battle zones.

So *Ephesians 6:10-18* is massively important. It is often viewed as an exciting and attractive picture of the Christian. We all like to feel it's US! It's the real me!

But to be honest, the real *me* is certainly not a mighty warrior standing confident and poised to apply the "coup de grace" to the enemy – regretfully, it's so often quite the contrary!

This is the reason why Paul exhorts, *"Finally, be strong in the LORD and in HIS mighty power. Put on the whole armour of GOD"*.

Without this armour of God, defeat is certain. Without the armour of God evil is bound to triumph. So this world without Christ lies in the power of the devil – ALL of it and it includes EVERY unregenerate person (*1 John 5:19*). John writes that the whole world is under the control of the evil one. The Authorised Version renders it, "the whole world lies in wickedness". It's like a pig lying in filth. It's covered in it. *Only soldiers of Christ can rise to the challenge.*

In *Ephesians 6:10* Paul is exclusively addressing believers – brothers in Christ. Nobody else has a hope of defeating Satan. Non believers have no defence at all even if they think they have: their weapons have no effect: they are wooden swords against ballistic missiles! Those not in Christ cannot defend themselves against the forces of darkness. They certainly cannot hope to attack them!

But you and I are in a different situation. Soldiers of Christ, arise and put HIS armour on! Here is the challenge. Is this what I want with all my heart? Enlisting in Christ's army means war whether I've bargained for it or not!

Chapter Nineteen

Getting priorities clear

What's in a name?

I had a nickname at school and I detested it! It was not complimentary, so I'm not about to tell you what it was! Mind you, some nicknames can be quite positive. There was a Jewish Christian who became a great friend of St. Paul whose name was Joseph. He hailed from Cyprus and was uncle to John Mark (who wrote the gospel account). We know him better by a nickname given him by Christians who knew him. They called him 'Barnabas', which means 'son of encouragement'. That Hebraism tells us that this particular Joseph had a massive reputation for being an encourager and there is evidence of this all through the Book of Acts. What a delightful nickname.

Our Lord gave some of his apostles intriguing nicknames. He called James and John "sons of thunder", perhaps indicating a certain tendency to violence. Some have wondered if they had at some stage been Zealots. After all, many young Galileans like them were engaged in the Jewish Underground movement against Rome.

Two of the Twelve bore the name Simon. One is designated 'Simon the Zealot' (*Luke 6:15*), so we have a good idea as to what his past was like. Jesus gave the other Simon the nickname 'Peter'. There is evidence that he too had a violent streak in him. Witness the fact that when in Jerusalem he carried a sword beneath his clothes (*John 18:10*). Zealots were always prepared for trouble: especially when in close proximity with Roman troops. Jerusalem was crawling with Roman soldiers at Festival times like Passover. Rome always feared Jewish revolt at the Feasts. Nationalist and religious emotions ran high, so the Roman presence in Jerusalem was always augmented during the Jewish Feasts. It is therefore understandable that any Zealot visiting the capital at Passover time would come ready for trouble. Peter's dexterity – he deftly sliced off a man's ear – shows that he was practised in handling a sword!

The nickname 'Peter' has a meaning. The Aramaic CEPHAS (*John 1:42*) means 'stone'. Its Greek equivalent is PETROS, meaning an **individual** stone – a small one like a piece of grit: just the thing to cause real irritation when trapped between your sandal and the sole of your foot!

The nickname suggests someone who could be very irritating! Certainly some of Peter's personality traits, impulsiveness and emotional swings might well have irritated his colleagues and possibly Jesus himself. Glimpses are provided in *Matthew 16:22-23* and also *Matthew 14:28; Mark 14:29; Luke 5:8* and *John 21:7*.

In spite of his irritating traits, Peter was used as heaven's spokesman when he uttered the inspired statement that Jesus owned as the foundation of his Church.

"On this rock I will build my Church" is a clear reference to the revelation, *"You are the Messiah (anointed King and Priest), the son of the living God!"* (*Matthew 16:16-18*). The word 'rock' there is PETRA, meaning a mighty rock: a dramatic contrast to Petros, meaning a small stone. Even an irritating disciple of Jesus can be used by God to speak out inspired truth! From a personal point of view, I'm glad about that!

Following his baptism in the Holy Spirit (*Acts 2:4*) Peter surrendered himself completely to the Word of God and the Holy Spirit. He became rock-solid in his standing for Christ and devoted himself to encourage others to stand firm.

True grit
In the closing period of his life, then a prisoner in Rome, Peter wrote to encourage believers and prepare them for escalating opposition. Scholars believe that his two letters date from 63AD, by which time both Jewish religion and Roman society had become violently opposed to Christians. Within a year, on July 19th in the year 64, the city of Rome would suffer a catastrophic fire: seriously damaging the city and destroying much of the central area. Initial blame was placed firmly upon the Emperor Nero, who was known to favour a remodelling of central Rome and who celebrated by playing a lyre and singing while watching the conflagration from a high tower. But the public hatred towards Christians and their gospel led to a shifting of blame to them. They were innocent of the charge but Nero was quick to make scapegoats of them. Without evidence the accusation still stuck fast.

The resulting suffering of the Roman church is legendary. Great numbers of believers were rounded up and publicly ripped apart in the arena by wild animals; some were bound to stakes, covered in pitch and burned as illumination in Nero's pleasure gardens.

This happened within a year of Peter's writing. He wrote from Rome in order to prepare Christians in the Provinces for what they might expect in the near future. Things were going from bad to worse in the Imperial capital and what was beginning in Rome would certainly spill over with lightning speed into the wider Empire. The truth was alarming, but Peter's grit and determination compelled him to write in love. It meant 'telling it like it is'!

The double edged sword of persecution
Scholars feel that when Peter refers to *"She who is in Babylon"* (*1 Peter 5:13*) he is referring in coded language to the church in Rome. He is writing from Rome. According to *1 Peter 1:1* Peter wrote to Christians in Asia Minor (modern Turkey). They needed strong encouragement to face dreadful events that would soon overtake them. A lesser man might have tried to persuade them to look on the bright side, but Peter loved the truth … even when it might cause distress. He spoke and wrote the truth in love and we have the privilege of receiving his letters in the same way his original readers did – with sober judgment, for we are facing very challenging days ourselves. Many are the signs that society has turned against the God of the Bible and his precious and unique Son, our Lord Jesus. Politically and socially Bible believing Christians are marginalised and considered fanatical.

It is superfluous to catalogue these anti-Christian antics because they are all too common and obvious. Suffice to say that we are well and truly in the time of trial that will precede the coming of the Lord. We anticipate the time of great glory, but we understand that the night of suffering must be endured before that day dawns.

The persecution Peter's friends faced and which we face is on two fronts. His first letter sets out to prepare believers for trouble from outside: from society, religious and political, Jewish and Roman. The second letter is weighted rather differently and deals with the attack upon truth coming from *inside* the churches. Peter speaks of false prophets and teachers who threaten to weaken the faith of believers by introducing notions that have no biblical substance.

Weakening your opponent from inside and thus setting him up for attack from outside is a good military stratagem. Infiltration and propaganda are used to weaken resolve and disguise danger. Defences come down. This inner weakening makes it far easier for the enemy to attack successfully. Satan is well aware of that and he operates accordingly.

If we fail to recognise his method we shall reap terrible consequences. The need to close ranks around the Bible has never been greater.

Preparation for war should focus our priorities. Peter was very clear on this when he wrote. He referred to a number of "precious" things. Some of these are predictable ... but not all.

Our precious Saviour
Peter says Jesus Christ is precious to God, is precious to Peter and precious to his readers (*1 Peter 2:4* and *7*). We are utterly devoted to Christ: we worship him as our Lord and Saviour. There is no other name under heaven given to men by which we must be saved (see *Acts 4:13*).

The precious blood of Christ
In *1 Peter 1:19* we have reference to the precious blood of our Saviour, shed to bring redemption. Peter is completely sold out to the Lamb of God, the One without blemish or defect who shed his blood on our behalf. The Cross is the crux of the matter for Peter and must be for us too.

Our precious faith
Even when highly refined, gold is not immune from fire. Our precious faith, though refined to the limit through suffering, will *never* perish but will result in praise, glory and honour when Jesus is revealed (*1 Peter 1:7; 2 Peter 1:1*). Religion and the world will threaten our faith – and are doing so – but by the Word and Spirit we stand resolute in the face of all opposition. As the Reformers insisted: "By Scripture alone, by faith alone, by grace alone, through Christ alone, to God's glory alone"!

God's precious promises
In *2 Peter 1:4*, Peter calls God's promises *"very great and precious"*. Is it not the simple truth? *Everything* rests on the faithful promises of God. Indeed, we might say they are commandments God lays upon himself! Nothing can shake them: we are completely secure in them whatever happens.

Because we are his children, participators in the divine nature, Gods's precious word is our guarantee.

But now, here is the surprise!

My precious wife
1 Peter 3:7 is a tremendous surprise. Of our wives Peter says, *"consider them precious"*. That is the literal meaning here. He uses the very same word that he uses of those other glorious priorities. Are we surprised?

How greatly do I value my wife, Lindy? Do I see her as the Lord's most glorious gift to me after my salvation? Do I value her and invest time and attention to blessing her above all else, cherishing her and building her up as a person as well as a disciple?

If the Lord spares us both, the strength of our marriage will be a critical factor in our standing strong against the wave of suffering that is on its way and a critical factor in the power of our prayer life.

Food for thought ... and action.

Chapter Twenty

Press on to know the Lord

Lindy and I are privileged to take groups of Christians to Israel several times each year. Whilst in Galilee we visit various ruined villages and towns that were thriving communities in New Testament times. Bethsaida, now in ruins, was a prominent centre of the fishing industry. It is located on the north east corner of the Sea of Galilee. Indeed, 'Beth-saida' means 'house (or site) of fishing'.

It's an exciting place to explore: its little streets and homes closely guarding their memories of golden days when Jesus of Nazareth ministered there.

Bethsaida witnessed remarkable miracles, but for all that the attitude of the residents tended towards indifference. Our Lord himself addressed their unbelief, *"Woe to you, Bethsaida! For if the miracles that were performed in you had been performed in Tyre and Sidon, they would have repented long ago, sitting in sackcloth and ashes. But it will be more bearable for Tyre and Sidon at the judgment than for you"* (*Luke 10:13-14*).

Among Bethsaida's more famous sons were three members of Jesus' inner band: Simon Peter, Andrew and Philip (*John 1:44*).

Philip's parents gave him a Greek name, Philippos, which suggests he was from a Hellenistic Jewish family. The influence of Greek culture was strong among Galilean Jews.

Philippos means 'horse-lover', but we have no means of telling why he was called that. I don't suppose his father was a bookie!

It is interesting that when a group of Greeks (presumably Hellenistic Jews) present in Jerusalem for Passover wished to see Jesus, it was Philip they singled out: *"Sir, we would like to see Jesus."* It was a trigger moment regarding our Lord's revelation of his glory. *"The hour has come for the Son of Man to be glorified"* (*John 12:20-23*).

Focus in the pulpit
I recall being confronted with that very same request when standing in a country pulpit many years ago and getting ready to preach. A card had been placed there with those very words, *"Sir, we would like to see Jesus!"* As I remember the moment, it still makes me uneasy. Was the congregation asking to see Jesus revealed in *me* or in *my message*? Either way it is a fixture in my memory and remains an enormous challenge, focusing my thinking dramatically whenever I preach. What am I really engaged in here? Am I here to educate, entertain, move, challenge … or am I here to reveal Jesus?

Revelation of Jesus comes about when the Holy Spirit anoints the message. The sermon lacks life and convicting power unless that happens.

Revelation of Jesus also comes through the testimony of the preacher's likeness to his Master. This is demonstrated in *Revelation 1:9*, where John tells us he was on the island of Patmos *"because of the word of God and the testimony of Jesus Christ."*

John's faithful proclamation of Jesus as Lord and Saviour came by means of the Scriptures and it was also proclaimed by the level of his Christ-likeness. Both were essential parts of John's life of faith and were the factors which led to his being sentenced by Rome to hard labour in the mineral mines on Patmos.

Here is a massive challenge to us: *John's testimony was as vital as his preaching*: his holy life empowered his preaching and his faithful exposition was confirmed in his holiness. But the focal point of both was Jesus himself.

Jesus fills the Bible
Many years ago, when I was a relatively new believer, a visiting preacher stood in our pulpit and, brandishing a New Testament, announced, *"This* is the Christian's Bible."

It rankled then and it infuriates me now. How could an Evangelical preacher and he a Minister at that – make such a crass statement? None of the church leaders present challenged the man and so the congregation filed out under the impression that for Christians the Old Testament was of far less importance than the New. This is such a serious lie that if we go with it our entire battle strategy as disciples called to spiritual warfare is compromised.

How do we proclaim Jesus? We do it by proclaiming him from the Bible. How did the apostles do it? By proclaiming him from the Bible. But which part of the Bible? The only part they had! There was not a single written book of the New Testament until at least two decades after Jesus ascended!

So the apostles' preaching of the gospel, confirmed by seeing astonishing victories over the kingdom of Satan, was the result of preaching Jesus from the Hebrew Scriptures and providing the supporting testimony of their changed lives and their personal experiences of the Lord!

In this they took their cue from Jesus himself. One of the most extraordinary Bible studies ever given took place on the open road. Luke describes it in his gospel account (*Luke 24:13-32*). Two disciples – Cleopas and a companion – were returning to their home at Emmaus, having been in Jerusalem for the Passover Feast. There they had witnessed the crucifixion of Jesus whom they had hoped was the Messiah come to deliver Israel from Rome. They shared this hope with many Jews who had high expectations of Jesus, only to have them dashed when he was arrested, tried and killed.

We cannot possibly appreciate the awestruck amazement of these two fellow travellers when the resurrected Jesus showed up and opened the Hebrew Scriptures to them, revealing *himself* in the prophecies and types. Their own words tell it best: *"Were not our hearts burning within us as he talked with us on the road and opened the Scriptures to us?"*

That very evening Jesus appeared to them again when they

were with the Eleven and some other disciples gathered in Jerusalem (*Luke 24:44-45*). Once again he opened up the Hebrew Scriptures, revealing himself with a clarity that was heart-stopping. He used *every section of the Scriptures* but did not include a single syllable of the New Testament for the simple reason that at that time it did not exist!

Note that he said, *"These are the words I spoke to you **while I was still with you**: Everything must be fulfilled that is written about me ...."*

It's clear therefore that in his disciple training, during the period leading up to his Passion, Jesus majored on the portions of Scripture that spoke of his messiahship: his eternal priesthood and kingship: his need to die as the sacrificial lamb before entering into his kingly glory.

What a fascinating glimpse into the way our Lord prepared his disciples for trouble.

Praise the Lord that we now have the glorious enrichment of the New Testament standing with the Hebrew Scriptures! The biblical revelation of Jesus thus provided prepares disciples to pass through personal crises of faith and also opposition from government, false religion and the forces of the devil. This is the core element in battle readiness. Without the centrality of Jesus in my life I cannot expect to stand in the time of trial.

You may think this obvious, but I know for myself how easily Jesus can be nudged out of the centre-spot. Other things take over and quite often it happens in all innocence.

It is quite possible for us to elevate *Church* to a status above Jesus. Does that shock you? Ask yourself, "How much time and attention have I devoted to church matters this week: attending meetings of various kinds and investing time in fellowship with the members?" Now here comes the challenge that impacts on me just as much as on you: make an honest assessment of quality time spent personally *in the presence of Jesus* this week. How do the two compare? Are you satisfied? Do you think Jesus is satisfied?

Then again, I can be obsessed with *knowledge*: devoting hours of my time to Bible research: increasing my knowledge of the Bible text, Bible background, doctrine: all done in order to make me a better preacher. But, whatever the motive, if those things take the place of knowing Jesus himself they have become idols.

As men and women who have been trained to think in a Greek way, we have a thirst for knowledge. As believers we have a thirst for knowledge about God: about Jesus: about the Holy Spirit: about doctrine. The Hebrew way, by contrast, is not to strive for knowledge *about* these things but rather be living in the reality of them. Knowing about Jesus is wonderful, but it cannot compare with knowing *him*!

As a preacher the terrible draw of Bible knowledge and precision of doctrine is so strong as to be virtually irresistible.

But that is the devil's trick: it is *not* irresistable. Adam swapped knowledge for relationship with God and it resulted in the Fall. Adam could have resisted the temptation, but he chose not to. That's frightening.

I must press on to know the Lord ... and so must you.

Back to the country
I have been a preacher for over half a century: faithfully proclaiming the word of God far and wide.

Many who know me consider me to be a mature Christian. Basing that consideration upon what? Basing it substantially upon my preaching and writing: my public ministry. That's all that most see because for many of them I am a bird of passage. Now you see me: now you don't! But is what they see and hear a true reflection? Is my *public* persona the *real* one? Does my ministry tell the whole story?

I began by speaking of that little country pulpit bearing the inscription, *"Sir, we want to see Jesus"*. Was that congregation asking to see Jesus revealed in *me* or in *my message*?

Whether they were aware of it or not, it must surely be *both*.

When I was a student at my theological college in Bristol, a great student friend gave me a Puritan quotation to fix to my study wall. I have it still. *"Thou art a preacher of the Word: mind thy business."*

I cannot speak for you, nor would I wish to, but I know for myself that this is the issue. Being a preacher I know a great

156

deal about Jesus and could hold you spellbound with what I have learned through my life. My years in theological college, lessons learned through church leadership, our many experiences in Israel … all have contributed to building my knowledge and understanding about the person and work of Jesus the Messiah. But my 'business' here below is to know **HIM**.

This is the way to victory.

Chapter Twenty one

A living testimony

I could sense her anguish in every word. Elisabeth lost her husband a dozen years ago but the ache is still in her heart. I knew John well. He was a remarkable disciple of Jesus and a well loved Vicar. Elisabeth has tried her level best to stay at St James' under the new, kindly Incumbent: but it has been painful. Every stone screams "John!" at her, and church members she once knew intimately and whose lives she and John had impacted switched allegiance to their new pastor and his wife the instant they arrived. Or so it seemed to Elisabeth, and it felt like rejection. To some extent it was inevitable but it was still jolly hard to take.

Elisabeth confided that she would love to leave the village. She has married sons who have settled miles away and although she would dearly love to live nearer, she has a dread of becoming a burden on them – and especially on her daughters in law.

Elisabeth says that she longs for pastures new. The question is where is the pasture? I suggested a location equidistant from her sons: close enough to be accessible yet distant enough to maintain her (and their) independence.

Elisabeth has been asking the Lord to take her to a greener pasture, but so far nothing has become clear. Maybe the Lord wants her to take some initiative herself. I suggested that her priority should be to locate a good church.

Find the church, *then* find the house. Elisabeth agrees. Regarding a church: she says her first priority is to find one with excellent Bible teaching. Her husband, John, was a man of the Word and she could never rest easy in a congregation where the pulpit ministry was less than thoroughly Evangelical.

I wanted to concur wholeheartedly. After all, I was trained in an Evangelical theological college and have been a Bible expositor for more than fifty years. I have always been a preacher of the Word and I have applied myself to my calling in as thorough a manner as possible. Of *course,* I reckoned, Elisabeth was right: finding a church with superb Bible teaching is her supreme need … or is it?

Truth to tell, Elisabeth (now pushing 8o) has had a lifetime of Bible teaching. First as a young Christian in her parents' home and home church and then at Bible College before meeting John and then sitting under his ministry for thirty five years. She has been well fed on the finest of fare.

I have no wish to be offensive or to be guilty of betraying my Evangelical roots, but the truth is that Bible teaching these days is available from sources other than the pulpit – much of it is superb. We all have access to recordings, books and the Internet, so teaching *per se* is not in short supply and some of us are positively obese with it: we stuff ourselves at every opportunity.

What cannot be experienced through the media, however, is true fellowship with other believers.

That is why the suggestion by some that you can have "a church without walls" is unhelpful. Church life without deep personal relationship and interaction with other true believers may seem attractive on the superficial level but it is woefully inadequate and cannot genuinely be called Church life at all.

One reason is that in order to be changed by the Word, we must submit to the refining work of the Spirit *through other believers.* This is picked up by James in his remarkable little letter: *"Therefore confess your faults to each other and pray for each other so that you may be made whole"* (*James 5:16*).

"To be like Jesus … all I ask, to be like him"
So my suggestion to Elisabeth was that she should search for people who are like Jesus. They are not hard to spot actually but in my experience they are rare. When you see one you know it straight away: but the honest truth is that it's rather like looking for the proverbial needle in a haystack! They take some finding, but when you succeed, you jolly well know it!

"You cynical blighter!" I hear you say. Sorry, but there it is. I do not believe there is virtue in being an optimist. Surely we are called to be *realists* and I confess that I do not see much Christ-likeness around. I long for the moment when people can look at *me* and know instinctively that I have been with

Jesus and am being visibly transformed through that relationship (see *Acts 4:13*).

We might argue that it is hard to identify loving churches from a distance: that you only *know* one when you're *in* one! But Jesus seems to suggest otherwise.

He actually said "all men" will identify true discipleship when they see genuine love at work among his disciples (*John 13:35*). Good news travels. We know of churches where there is good teaching and churches where there are claims of 'signs and wonders' … but what of groups of believers known for the quality of their love and their Christ-likeness? If that is what Jesus was talking about, it may give a powerful clue to why we seem to be so ineffective.

Right doctrine is only right biblically when it is visibly authenticated by my changed life. Mere doctrine by itself – however precise – is not true Christian faith at all: it is empty religion. It might be dead right … but it's still dead!

Facts of the Apostles
Acts 2:42 is one of those statements that sets the agenda for disciples of Christ. The 3000 new believers committed themselves to
  - the apostles' doctrine
  - the fellowship
  - the breaking of bread
  - the prayers

First up is *"the apostles' doctrine"*. This refers to the *substance* of the teaching rather than to the *activity* of teaching. They were not so much enthusiasts for preach-**ing**, but for the preached word itself.

That, it seems to me, is a very important distinction. There is a tendency amongst some Christians to form preachers' fan clubs.

The preacher might be a local Pastor, a travelling Bible teacher, a broadcaster or a writer, but if his gift for communication sparkles he will have a following. I know of people who will travel miles in order to hear the latest offering from their favourite preacher. But that is not what *Acts 2:42* is describing! It was devotion to the *substance* of the preaching. But for what purpose? Was it in order to stuff the memory with doctrine or was there a higher purpose? Surely that higher purpose was determination to *live* by the Word rather than simply to know it.

Allow me to pose a question. How many churches do you know of where good teaching is the main feature? Now permit me to ask a further question: how many do you know of where changed lives are the main feature?

You might say, "Well, we cannot look into people's hearts so we cannot say if they have changing lives." Is that not sheer nonsense? It was not so much precision of doctrine that made the disciples recognisable, it was Christ-like lives. Evidence of Christ in my changed life is what people need to *see* in me much more than the excellence of my Bible knowledge and preaching.

Although correct doctrine is a critical matter, our Lord never placed supreme emphasis upon correct doctrine. He placed it on walking in fellowship with God and with one another. Indeed, his statement recorded in *John 13:35* puts it clearly: *"By this all men will know that you are my disciples, **if you love one another**."* Doctrinal correctness is not the clearest mark of a disciple, rather it is the application of the Word that shrieks to the world, "Here is a man in Christ! Look, his changing life is the reality of the Christian faith!"

At the close of the Sermon on the Mount, that momentous teaching seminar on true discipleship, our Lord punches the doctrine home with, *"Therefore everyone who hears these words of mine **and puts them into practice** is like a wise man who built his house on a rock."* (*Matthew 7:24*)

Then again, in *John 14:21*, Jesus thumps the truth into the disciples: *"Whoever has my words [doctrine] AND obeys them [changed life], he is the one who loves me."*

We may add further statements:

"Be doers of the Word and not hearers only". (*James 1:22*)

"Dear children, let us not love with words or tongue but with actions and in truth. This, then, is how we know that we belong to the truth, and how we set our hearts at rest in his presence whenever our hearts condemn us." (*1 John 3:18-20*)

Whilst correct doctrine is indispensable and must be fought for and maintained, of greater importance is personal holiness, shared life and expressed love. Doctrine is massively important, but application of the Word to life is much more so.

We have been severely influenced by Greek thinking as against Hebrew thinking (the mind-set of Jesus). Greek thinking elevates the mind, Hebrew the heart. What I believe is one thing, what I am becoming is quite another. ***

In writing to the believers in Corinth Paul was conscious of the imbalance we are speaking of. We'll give him the last word. In *1 Corinthians 4:16-20*, he wrote,
*"Therefore I urge you to imitate me (*as he himself imitated Christ*). For this reason I am sending to you Timothy, my son whom I love, who is faithful in the Lord.* **He will remind you of my way of life in Christ Jesus, which agrees with what I teach everywhere and in every church.** *Some of you have become arrogant, as if I were not coming to you. But I will come to you very soon, if the Lord is willing, and* **then I will find out not only how these arrogant people are talking, but what power they have. For the Kingdom of God is not a matter of talk but of power."**

And so it is!

*** See overleaf

***Brilliant exposure of the way Greek thinking has infiltrated and poisoned the Church and how we may counteract it may be found in three volumes by Steve Maltz.

- "How the Church lost the Way"
- "How the Church lost the Truth"
- "To Life"

All are available from C L Ministries (address on the back cover of this book).
Individual volumes are £12.00 each plus Postage, but all three may be purchased (Post Free in the UK) for £35.00.

Chapter Twenty two

Truly devoted

Isn't it remarkable to discover new depths of revelation in familiar Bible passages? To discover the deepest treasures, deep digging is required. This can involve hard work and is often a lengthy process!

A Eureka-moment

You can sometimes be surprised. I consider myself pretty familiar with the contents of *Acts 2*, but quite recently, when reading it for the umpteenth time, I had a "Eureka- moment"! I came across something that struck me as odd and, all of a sudden, it gleamed out at me!

One of the most challenging descriptions provided by Luke in the Book of Acts (what I like to refer to as "The Facts of the Apostles"!) nestles snugly in his description of the Feast of Pentecost. We are provided not only with a graphic description of the moment when the apostles were drenched inside and out with the Holy Spirit, but also with a clear account of Peter's evangelistic sermon. The 3000 Jewish responders expressed their new birth in a set of new priorities: *"They devoted themselves to the apostles' doctrine and to the fellowship, to the breaking of bread and the prayers" (Acts 2:42).*

All familiar stuff providing a helpful insight into the priorities of those first believers. The Greek word "devoted" is very strong and it carries the idea of passionate continuity: never giving up.

That I already knew, but what lit up for me was the first item of Luke's list: *"They devoted themselves to the apostles' doctrine ... ,"* That is to say, the *content or substance* of the apostles' message.

True discipleship involves *living* in biblical truth: not simply paying lip-service to it!

Reading the small print
But notice *precisely* what Luke wrote. He referred to *"the apostles' doctrine"*. What is that? Well, let me say what it is *not*: it is not the developed doctrine of Augustine or even Luther and Calvin! How could it be? The apostles lived centuries before those worthies did their systematic work.

But more than that, Luke cannot include Paul! Paul came to faith well after the events on the Temple Mount described by Luke in *Acts 2*.

So why is this important? Because it shows that the first believers devoted themselves to the doctrine taught to the *original* apostles. That is to say, those apostles that physically accompanied Jesus throughout his ministry, up to and beyond the crucifixion. Luke can only be referring to that limited band.

Paul was not among them, but that is not to demean the glorious revelation that was later given through him. According to *2 Peter 3:16* Paul's writings have the authority of Scripture and were acknowledged as such from the very start. However, we have to place the emphasis for basic Christianity further back to the original teaching provided by the Lord himself. That is what the Twelve were exposed to. This is what Paul sought to express and develop later on when he came to write his letters, but *Acts 2:42* cannot include those. Luke presents us with a more primitive form of belief in Jesus. But quite plainly it was primary because it was the pure doctrine of Jesus himself.

Learners and followers
Peter and the others devoured that doctrine. It is implicit in the meaning of "disciple" (Greek: *math<u>e</u>t<u>e</u>s,* meaning "learner and follower"). But what was the doctrine they learned and lived?

First, we acknowledge that high priority was given by the Lord to the fulfilment of the Hebrew Scriptures. *Luke 24:27* and *44* are very revealing. Jesus said, *"These are the words I spoke to you **while I was still with you**: everything must be fulfilled that is written about me in the Law of Moses, the Prophets and the Psalms."* Here Jesus indicates that a vast amount of his disciple training had to do with the fulfilment of the "Old Testament": and fulfilment in *him*! He hammered home the vital importance of the Hebrew Scriptures as the basis for the gospel and for the life of faith. The prophecies and types of Jesus were fundamental and without them it would not be possible to evangelise the world. Indeed, when our Lord breathed the Holy Spirit into the apostles in the Upper Room it was to open their minds to understanding the Scriptures as they pointed to him (*John 20:22; Luke 24:45*).

To this we can confidently add the Kingdom teaching exemplified in the Sermon on the Mount, the "I am" sayings recorded by John, the need for rebirth recorded in *John 3*, the apocalyptic teaching as recorded in *Matthew 24* and *25*, truths concerning the person and ministry of God the Father and the Holy Spirit in *John 14 – 16*, the power of love in *John 13*; indeed, *everything* contained in the four Gospel accounts. But the straightforward teaching found in the Gospel accounts is a far cry from the intricacies of systematic theology laid down through following centuries which was so heavily influenced by Greek methodology.

I recall a humorous anecdote provided by a former student of Swiss theologian Karl Barth. Karl Barth was the author of one of the best regarded works of theology entitled, "Church Dogmatics". It is a set of voluminous tomes. An impertinent student once asked, "Dr Barth, do you believe you are going to Heaven?" To which Barth responded, "Good question! Let me tell you how it will be. When I approach Heaven's entrance and the gatekeepers see me coming, I expect one will say to the other, 'Karl Barth is due in today, and here he comes, pushing a wheelbarrow filled with his thirteen books of Church Dogmatics!' The other gatekeeper will chuckle and say, 'Well, *he's* welcome but he can leave what's in the wheelbarrow right here by the gate!'"

Some have said that many of history's wars and cruelties result from the Church's theology. I dare say that is so. Groups of "Christians" dug into their trenches, lobbing theological grenades across No-man's-Land, seeking to destroy each other in the name of Truth. At certain times spiritual grenades have been swapped for military ones. The tendency is there even within today's Church communities.

That includes Evangelical and Charismatic groupings, sad to say.

Which theology?
But which theology is used in these volatile encounters? Is it the simplicity that is in Christ or is it that web of systematic theology, spun by generations of ecclesiastical brain-boxes, some of them not truly spiritual men at all?

Throughout the centuries there have been men and women who have had such intense love for Jesus and for people that, when confronted with the labyrinth of theology standing between them and Jesus, they have kicked over the theological traces and embraced a simple life style and a simplified faith.

There are biblical antecedents. Consider how Jewish people in Jesus' day were treated by their religious leaders when they opted out from observing the "Traditions of the Elders". These God-fearing Jewish people had a longing for God and his Word, but could not cope with what was laid on them by legalistic Rabbis who had added a massive amount of religious tradition to the pure Scriptures. Those religious leaders branded such rebels as "sinners" and wrote them off as being beyond the pale.

It is significant that our Lord invested hours of his time with these so-called "sinners" (see *Matthew 9:10-13; Luke 15:1-2 et al*) and castigated the leaders for their folly in adding religious tradition to God's pure Word (*Matthew 15:2-9; Mark 7:8*).

The religious leaders had created a situation in which decent God-fearing people were barred from Temple and synagogue because they could not submit to such religious cant and dogma. But it went further than that. Many of these "sinners" were led to believe that they were beyond the reach of God, because if they did not come to him through the maze of Rabbinic Judaism, they could not approach him at all. That is what they were encouraged to believe. Jesus had compassion and reached out to them with grace to put the record straight.

Before he came to Christ, Paul was a religious Jew of the deepest dye. He had perpetrated these pious yet non-biblical traditions (*Galatians 1:14*) and in *Colossians 2:8* he goes as far as to link them with demonic spirits. Astonishing discernment from a man formerly steeped in such tradition himself.

Revelation 18

In the amazing vision recorded by John in *Revelation 18*, he sees the fall of Babylon the Great. Generally acknowledged as the satanically controlled world order this "Babylon" includes anything that is not under the authority of Jesus. It may fairly be said to include "human tradition" (see again the confirming Scripture, *Colossians 2:8*). That being said, the command of the angel to *"come out of her, my people"* has tremendous resonance, has it not?

As the coming of Jesus approaches, we are already facing the fight of our lives. Satan is on the march. Overcoming him will not happen by default, that's for sure. To ignore or be unaware of the battle is no guarantee of safety: quite to the contrary! It is to court certain disaster.

The history of the Christian denominations reveals a tough truth. It is possible to hear the clarion call, *"come out of her, my people"*, and to obey the call by coming out of tradition into the freedom of believing and living the Bible way – the *Jesus* way – only to shrink back at some later stage when, for whatever reason, the going gets tough. It often happens when the original "movers and shakers" have been replaced. Those with the vision pass on the baton, only for it to be fumbled and dropped.

That pattern of renewal is common in the history of the Church as it has recognised and recoiled from the shackles of religious tradition and moved out for the sake of biblical truth and the freedom and life of the Holy Spirit. It motivated the Lollards, the Reformers, the Baptists, the Wesleyans, the Brethren, the Salvationists, the Pentecostalists, the Charismatic Movement ... the list is long.

But something has happened with monotonous regularity. Within a very short space of time, religious tradition has invaded and strangled the life out of the renewal. Sometimes old traditions rear their ugly heads while at other times new traditions come grinning. Either way the freshness of Heaven's life is stifled and it's "As you were".

Can we not see the hand of Satan here? Is human (religious) tradition not the work of demons?

So I'm a Cynic, am I? I wish it were so for then I could confess my fault and move on. The *status quo* could be maintained and we could all carry on regardless.

However, I have this uneasy feeling that my "Eureka moment" when confronted with *Acts 2:42* was a moment of truth. Where we go from here is anybody's guess ... but surely it must be *somewhere*?

Chapter Twenty three

"Together we stand ..."

When Jesus gave his stirring call to arms in the shadow of mighty Mount Hermon (*Matthew 16:18*) it was a clarion call to his corporate body: the Church.

"... on this rock I will build my Church, and the gates of Hell will not overcome it."

We have already seen that the word *"gates"* stands for *"authorities"* and the phrase *"will not overcome it"* can also be translated *"will not be able to withstand it."* This is fighting talk showing that the Church Jesus builds will have power and authority to defend itself against the forces of the devil and also power and authority to attack and destroy the works of the devil.

"Church" (*ekklesia*) refers to the gathered community of believers under the rule of the Lord. The implication is clear: if we are functioning as true Church we can be sure of victory ... but not unless.

Spiritual warfare is a corporate business. True, Satan delights to invade our space as individual warriors, but as long as we are standing with each other and full-square on the Word of God our vulnerability is drastically reduced.

An unlikely foundation for fellowship!

The second apostolic journey of Paul was a great adventure. Luke (the author of Acts) describes it in meticulous detail. Paul entered mainland Europe after a sequence of remarkable and unexpected promptings of the Holy Spirit. It was only after several abortive attempts to evangelise other areas that Paul was led to the European city of Philippi. This important city enjoyed the status of a Roman colony and had a prosperous Greek population. Paul, Silas and Luke had left Asia Minor under the clear (and frustrating) strategy of the Holy Spirit who now pitched the trio into a true but unanticipated adventure of faith that threatened their very lives (*Acts 16:6-40*)!

As usual, Paul's first act was to seek out the resident Jews, of whom it seems there were very few, and he conducted an *ad hoc* evangelistic meeting by the River Gangites. If ten Jewish men were present in a town they could establish a synagogue. If less, the Jews met at a Place of Prayer near flowing (living) water. Such was the case here. Indeed, no men are mentioned at all: Luke simply refers to women (*Acts 16:13*).

The first converts in Philippi were certainly an assorted bunch! *Acts 16* tells of Lydia, the Jewish business woman (*14-15*), a nameless girl who had been demonised but to whom Paul ministered deliverance (*16-18*) and a hard-nosed ex-legionary who was rewarded with the job of town jailer (*27-34*). Hardly a promising group to form the founding members of a church! But under the amazing hand of God, the church that grew from that unlikely beginning became a byword for loving fellowship of the most rugged kind.

Follow the leader

A careful reading of Acts 16 shows that the writer of Acts was present during Paul's ministry in Philippi, having joined Paul at Troas. The word "we" shows this. The writer was Luke whom Paul described as the "well loved doctor" (*Colossians 4:14*).

Luke never refers to himself before 16:10. He is in on the action throughout Acts 16, and then the word "they" appears again in *Acts 16:40*. This suggests that Luke stayed behind to continue the work in Philippi. His warm, generous pastoral gifts that made him the "well loved doctor" were focused on the young church in Philippi. His efforts were amply rewarded in the establishment of a church that exuded joy and *fellowship*.

What is fellowship?

This is a critically important question when we are contemplating a Church that is being built for battle. If we are not standing strong in fellowship, we are not standing at all and defeat is a certainty.

When we look closely at the letter Paul wrote to the Philippians from gaol several years after his visit, we discover remarkable evidence that Luke's pastoral leadership had a powerful impact.

Some have called Philippians, "Paul's love letter to the churches"! The reason for this is not hard to find. Paul wrote most of his epistles to address life-style problems or to correct doctrine. However, apart from what appears to be a temporary "tiff" between two of the women members (*Philippians 4:2*), the church at Philippi is given a clean bill of health. So much so that the quality of their life together glows from every sentence. Paul is *thrilled* with them.

No wonder. The Philippian believers had become models in true body life: examples of the way it should be done! In no way is this more obvious than in their understanding of "fellowship". It's very different from what we might suppose!

Ask many Christians to describe "Fellowship" and they may well say something like, "Well, it is meeting one another and being happy together: it's that warm and cosy feeling we enjoy when we're together in the life of the church." Sometimes the word is used as a synonym for "meeting", in the sense of "The Women's Fellowship; the Men's Fellowship, the Young People's Fellowship and even the Choir Fellowship". In order to give what we do a bit of extra spiritual beef, we may speak of the Prayer Fellowship (much more spiritual that the Prayer *Meeting*, don't you think?).

Friends returning from holiday may well speak of a Church they attended as having wonderful fellowship because they were given a hand-shake, a smile and a coffee … maybe even a biscuit too!

The real thing

So what *is* fellowship? It is a translation of the Greek *koinonia*.

In his opening to the letter (*Philippians 1:4-5)* Paul says,

"In all my prayers for all of you, I always pray with joy because of your partnership (koinonia)in the gospel from the first day until now."

"... in the gospel" is better translated *"in your proclamation of the good news"*. In other words, they were completely at one with Paul and with each other in ministering the gospel to their community. They did not hold back and leave it to those "specially called". They were exercising the ministry gifts with a passion for evangelism ... and they were *all* engaged.

That is biblical fellowship, Philippians style! How about it?

Paul uses the word again a few verses later (7), where he writes,
"It is right for me to feel this way about all of you, since I have you in my heart; for whether I am in chains or defending and confirming the gospel, all of you share in God's grace with me."

Here is moving testimony to the Philippians' readiness to identify with Paul all the time, whether he was exercising his successful, up front preaching work or languishing in gaol (as he now was)! That word *"share"* is *"sunkoinonoi"*. Paul acknowledges that the Philippians are sharing with him in suffering and conflict and also in the grace of God in spite of distance parting them. Theirs was not fair-weather fellowship: it was unshakeable in every circumstance! He might be out of sight, but he certainly wasn't out of mind.

Am I ready to stand alongside you when I discover that in certain matters you are a prisoner to your own weaknesses? Or do I quietly withdraw? Then again, what will happen when you are being literally pilloried or imprisoned for your faith (it's coming soon)? Will I stand aloof or alongside?

It's a wonderful thing when I can say concerning you, "You touch *his* life, you touch *mine*. We stand together through thick and thin!"

That is biblical fellowship, Philippians style! How about it?

In Philippians 4:14 we have a real *coup de gras*. Paul uses that word *sunkoinonoi* again and this time it may even be more of a problem to us. It deals with sharing money and possessions! It has been said that the last thing to be converted in a believer is his pocket!

We might wonder if the Christians at Philippi were particularly prosperous, so that they had money to spare. The truth is different.

When Paul wrote to the Corinthians, the Macedonian believers (that includes the Philippians) were in desperate financial straits (*2 Corinthians 8:1-5*). He speaks in dramatic style of their "*most severe trial*" and their "*extreme poverty*", and yet this contrasts so markedly with their "*overflowing joy* and *rich generosity*". It gets quite embarrassing when Paul says they "*gave beyond their ability*" and "*urgently pleaded for the privilege of giving*".

A further noteworthy fact is that the beneficiaries of the Philippian largesse that Paul refers to were Jewish believers in distant Jerusalem, whose sense of superiority was well known to Gentile churches like Philippi. It made no difference. These were brothers in need and the Philippians rose to the challenge. So, taken together with *Philippians 4:14-16*, we are confronted with extraordinary and transformed life styles. No wonder Paul rated them so highly.

That is biblical fellowship, Philippians style! How about it?

Built for battle?
Facing the enemy requires strategic thinking ... and fighting. We shall not easily achieve our objectives so long as we retreat into our trenches and lie low.

Having to go "over the top" was always a ghastly prospect in war. The sweat and tears of anticipation were rapidly mixed with blood when the action started. You can't blame some troops who became paralysed with fear at the prospect.

Confrontation with the enemy and his henchmen is now a certainty for all of us. Our Lord spoke of it frequently and for a good many it has become their daily experience. We cannot say we have not been warned.

But what do we do? Surely we need to start by moving out from behind our barricades. For some it will be a denominational barricade; for others the barricade will be their home; for others their circle of friends and family.

The battle cry of *Psalm 68:1* needs to echo around our churches once again,
"May God arise, may his enemies be scattered; may his foes flee before him!"

That's fighting talk because when God arises to deal with his enemies he tends to use his troops to engage alongside him!

Are we ready? Let's go!

Selected Books by Chris Hill ...

"Speak, Lord!" ... But who's listening?

Apostasy is here! It grips many churches and individuals. Society is becoming increasingly opposed to biblical faith. Hatred of God is widespread and gaining ground. How do disciples of Christ prepare for trouble?

In this challenging and stimulating book, Chris Hill points the way forward through and beyond the time of trouble into the true glories that lie ahead. *£10.00 plus post and packing*

Elijah

Facing up to an increasingly hostile society and apostate Church requires guts and an iron determination to be faithful to Christ above all else. The example of Elijah is a powerful and inspiring encouragement to stand firm in the face of terrifying opposition from the most exalted quarters, both religious and secular. True prophetic living needs true prophetic examples. In this regard Chris Hill believes Elijah stands supreme!

£10.00 plus post and packing

The Real World of the New Testament

Chris Hill's fifty years of study and his frequent visits to Israel provide him with rare insights into the life and times of Bible characters. Here you will find a helpful historical overview and a penetrating analysis of the influence of Greece and Rome upon the Jews and the early Christians. Family life and the world of work are examined in detail, with particular reference to the fishing industry on the Sea of Galilee. Let the Bible come to life for you! *£10.00 plus post and packing*

The Letters of Peter

When the Church comes under attack from forces outside, it usually follows a period of softening up from within. This is the strategy of Satan and is clearly discernible in many churches today. The Church becomes weakened through wrong belief, deception and a lack of holiness and is set up for the ravages of persecution. In his two letters Peter addresses this problem head-on. How do we deal with false teachers and how do we face persecution? Chris Hill maintains that Peter's letters are truly tracts for our times. *£10.00 plus post and packing*

Selected DVDs and CDs by Chris Hill ...

The Land well loved (DVD set)

Chris Hill is acknowledged as one of the most experienced Israel Tour leaders in Britain, having led 90 tours during the last 30 years. His approach is decidedly Bible based and Jesus centred: every opportunity is taken to expound the Scriptures in the places where biblical events took place and great teaching was given.

This series of five DVDs (lasting 2 hours each) is a filmed record of Chris and Lindy Hill's May 2010 tour. Every leg of the journey was recorded and every word of his teaching included. The teaching is rich in Hebrew background information and is truly inspirational, conveying the depth and drama in the wonderful life and ministry of the Lord Jesus and his disciples.

The series will be welcomed by many hundreds of people who have accompanied Chris and Lindy on their Israel tours. The programmes are ideal for personal study and also for group home meetings.

The filming took place 'on the hoof', and in consequence skilfully preserves the immediacy of the moment.   *£30.00 plus post and packing*

Get Ready! (CD set)

The theme of this set of three CDs is preparation. "Get ready for trouble ... get ready for joy!" We must prepare for the return of Jesus and also for the dark and difficult days that will precede it. Chris Hill believes that, as in all else, Jesus sets the pace as the pioneer and perfecter of our faith. We look to Him. The Word of the Lord enables disciples to face the future by looking to Jesus and rejoicing in the blessed assurance that comes as a result!   *£9.00 plus post and packing*

Spiritual Warfare (CD set)

In this detailed exposition of Matthew 16:18-19, Chris Hill reveals an astonishing fact. The Church Jesus builds is in *permanent conflict* with Satan. Spiritual Warfare is the normal experience of true disciples of Jesus Christ because it was *His* normal experience! We look to Him to show us how to stand in the conflict. Jesus has promised to build His Church in such a way that victory is assured ... but only if we allow Him to build it *His* way!   *£6.00 plus post and packing*

Why not join Chris and Lindy Hill on one of their renowned Bible tours of
Israel?

Experience gained through over thirty years of leading Israel tours makes Chris one of today's foremost tour leaders. He and Lindy have led ninety tours during those years and several thousand people have joined them. Many of these folks return for a second tour! Some, indeed, have been with the Hills on as many as *five* occasions!

Scheduled flights, excellent hotels and coaches, together with a highly experienced Jewish Guide, guarantee a secure and rich experience. Chris's Bible teaching in each location visited brings the Word of God to life and the whole memorable experience enriches the faith of those who come.

Publications and Tour brochures available from

C L Publications

28 Thorney Road, Capel St Mary, Suffolk IP9 2LH
Tel: 01473 311128   Email: clministries@btinternet.com
www.clministries.org.uk